CARBON CONUNDRUM

How to Save Climate Change Policy from Government Failure

PHILIP BOOTH
CARLO STAGNARO

Institute of
Economic Affairs

T0002693

First published in Great Britain in 2022 by
The Institute of Economic Affairs
2 Lord North Street
Westminster
London SW1P 3LB
in association with London Publishing Partnership Ltd
www.londonpublishingpartnership.co.uk

The mission of the Institute of Economic Affairs is to improve understanding of the fundamental institutions of a free society by analysing and expounding the role of markets in solving economic and social problems.

A CIP catalogue record for this book is available from the British Library.

ISBN 978-0-255-36812-4

Many IEA publications are translated into languages other than English or are reprinted. Permission to translate or to reprint should be sought from the Director General at the address above.

Typeset in Kepler by T&T Productions Ltd
www.tandtproductions.com

Printed and bound in Great Britain by CMP UK

Carbon Conundrum

CONTENTS

Philip Booth

Philip Booth is Professor of Finance, Public Policy and Ethics at St. Mary's University, Twickenham. He also holds the position of Director of Catholic Mission at St. Mary's having previously been Director of Research and Public Engagement and Dean of the Faculty of Education, Humanities and Social Sciences. Philip was also Director of the Vinson Centre for the Public Understanding of Economics and Professor of Economics at the University of Buckingham for 2021–22. From 2002 to 2022, Philip was Academic and Research Director (previously, Editorial and Programme Director) at the IEA and then Senior Academic Fellow. From 2002 to 2015 he was Professor of Insurance and Risk Management at Cass Business School. He is a Senior Research Fellow in the Centre for Federal Studies at the University of Kent and Adjunct Professor in the School of Law, University of Notre Dame, Australia. Previously, Philip worked for the Bank of England as an adviser on financial stability issues and he was also Associate Dean of Cass Business School and held various other academic positions at City University. He has written widely, including a number of books, on investment, finance, social insurance and pensions as well as on the relationship between Catholic social teaching and economics. He is Deputy Editor of *Economic*

Affairs. He is a Fellow of the Royal Statistical Society, a Fellow of the Institute of Actuaries and an honorary member of the Society of Actuaries of Poland. He has previously worked in the investment department of Axa Equity and Law and was been involved in a number of projects to help develop actuarial professions and actuarial, finance and investment professional teaching programmes in Central and Eastern Europe. He has a BA in economics from the University of Durham and a PhD from City University.

Carlo Stagnaro

Carlo Stagnaro is research and studies director of Istituto Bruno Leoni, a Milan-based think tank. Before that he was chief of the Minister's Technical Staff at the Italian Ministry of Economic Development. He has an MSc in environmental engineering from the University of Genoa and a PhD in economics, markets, institutions from IMT Alti Studi – Lucca. Carlo is a member of the IEA's Academic Advisory Council as well as a research fellow of Epicenter, a fellow of the Italian Observatory on Energy Poverty and a member of the editorial board of the magazines *Energia* and *Aspenia*. For the IEA he wrote *Power Cut? How the EU Is Pulling the Plug on Electricity Markets* (2015). His latest book is *Molte Riforme per Nulla* (Marsilio, 2022), written with Alberto Saravalle. He is an economic columnist for the Italian daily magazine *Il Foglio*. He is on Twitter @CarloStagnaro.

SUMMARY

- Both the UK and the EU have made commitments to achieve carbon neutrality by 2050. Political leaders all over the world have promised 'new green deals' that involve embracing large-scale government intervention. These policies lead to substantial resources being allocated on the basis of politicians' own technological preferences, rather than according to the principles of economic and technical efficiency.
- Energy sources are both taxed and subsidised. In principle, environmental taxes and subsidies should reflect externalities. However, in practice, policy is chaotic with tax treatment reflecting the nature of the fuel, who consumes the fuel and for what purpose the fuel is used. In some countries, renewable energy receives large subsidies with little or no regard to the environmental benefit they actually deliver. Furthermore, fossil fuels are generally subsidised too. In the UK, that happens by an exemption from the general rate of value added tax.
- On average, oil products are taxed at €405 per tonne of oil equivalent in the UK and €334 in the EU27, as compared with €135 and €101 for natural gas and €112 and €84 for coal. This is despite the fact that coal, not

oil, poses the largest environmental challenges as far as climate change is concerned.

- Energy sources, including those that are taxed and including fossil fuels, are also heavily subsidised. In 2018 energy subsidies were as high as €500 per head in the UK and €355 in the EU27. Most subsidies were given to renewable energy sources, the production of which was subsidised by €448 per tonne of oil equivalent on average in the UK and €320 in the EU27. Subsidies were higher for solar photovoltaics (€1,468 per tonne of oil equivalent in the UK and €2,019 in the EU27), followed by wind power (€961 and €743, respectively). Hydro power and bio-energies received, on average, much lower subsidies. These differential subsidies to different forms of renewable energy sources are wasteful and inefficient. Subsidies to fossil fuels were generally intended to support consumption rather than production. On average, oil, natural gas and coal received €130, €61 and €86 per tonne of oil equivalent in subsidies in the UK and €320, €47 and €27 respectively in the EU27.

- If we net off taxes and subsidies, we find that, on balance, renewables are heavily subsidised, while fossil fuels have greater taxes levied on them than they receive in subsidies. However, there is no coherent pattern. The net effect of taxes and subsidies leads to substantially greater net taxes on oil than on natural gas while coal is taxed the least. The level of net taxes on energy sources does not, in any way, relate to the externalities from the energy source.

- If the EU-sponsored estimates of external costs from energy sources is taken as a benchmark, it can be said that all energy sources are either under-taxed or over-subsidised.
- It is clear that taxes and subsidies on energy sources are not designed as a rational tool of environmental policy. They are part of a broader industrial policy that reflects the individual preferences of policymakers and the producer and consumer interest groups that influence them.
- This means that current green policies are more costly than they need be. A rational system that taxed energy sources according to the damage caused by their emissions would ensure that greater levels of carbon reduction would be possible for a much lower economic cost. It would also make use of decentralised information, as individuals would be able to reduce carbon emissions in the way that was least costly for them.
- Climate change is by no means the only externality from the use of energy. Many other externalities have a local, not a global, nature. The problems are not significantly different from a range of other scenarios where economic activity by one party has an impact on another party. Externalities with a local impact do not justify either taxes or subsidies at the national level. They require a legal, institutional and constitutional framework which allows the maximum scope for preferences to be expressed through various bargaining and charging mechanisms at the local level.

- Decarbonisation has been established as a key policy objective for the UK and the EU. Economic efficiency, including efficiency of capital allocation, are especially important in this process given the immense costs involved. For this reason, the government should stop its policies of trying to pick winners, subsidising fossil fuels and subsidising renewables and levy a carbon tax proportional to emissions. Estimates of the damage caused by emissions may vary and those used by the EU are contestable. Thus, there is room for debate on how big a carbon tax should be. However, this is the most efficient mechanism available for reducing carbon emissions.
- The proceeds of a carbon tax should be used directly to reduce the tax burden in other areas. Welfare benefits would be uprated as a result of the impact of a carbon tax on prices. The aim of a carbon tax is to price carbon and not to increase the tax burden.
- The invasion of Ukraine by Russia does not change the argument. Indeed, it makes it more important that we adopt policies that lead to the efficient consumption and production of energy.

TABLES AND FIGURES

1   INTRODUCTION

Climate change: the political context

Since 24 February 2022, when Russian troops invaded Ukraine, all countries – particularly the UK and the EU member states – found themselves faced with a trade-off between energy security and decarbonisation. At least in the short run, energy security required governments to overlook their environmental targets, for example by maximising the output of coal-fired power plants in order to reduce the demand for natural gas. In the long run, though, all reiterated and reinvigorated their commitment to substantially cut the emissions of greenhouse gases (GHGs) and to achieve carbon neutrality by 2050. Decarbonisation, indeed, has been the main pillar of the UK's and Europe's environmental and energy policy for two decades. After the Covid-19 crisis it also became a driver, however misguided, of various relief and recovery packages by building upon previous grand plans to spur economic growth by promoting public and private investments in the field of sustainability.

Over a year earlier, on 18 November 2020, UK Prime Minister, Boris Johnson, released a ten-point plan to achieve carbon neutrality by 2050. The ambition is that, by then, Britain's net emissions of carbon dioxide and other GHGs would be brought down to zero and its contribution to global climate change will be eradicated accordingly.

According to its proponents, the plan 'will mobilise £12 billion of government investment to create and support up to 250,000 highly-skilled green jobs in the UK, and spur over three times as much private sector investment by 2030'.[1] Mr Johnson's blueprint has been dubbed a 'green industrial revolution' and sets ambitious goals regarding the development and deployment of specific technologies. Moreover, it aims to improve energy efficiency and increase use of renewable energy in residential as well as in industrial buildings, protect and enhance the natural environment, promote research and development in clean fuels and technologies, and make the City of London the global centre of green finance.

The European Union is pursuing its own 'green industrial revolution'. It is planning to achieve carbon neutrality by 2050, and a substantial reduction in carbon emissions of 55 per cent by 2030 compared with a 1990 baseline.[2] Under the plan, measures will be taken at EU and national levels to achieve the decarbonisation of several major production processes, the increased use of renewable energies and greater energy efficiency. In Brussels, as well as in other European capitals, they have a clear idea of

---

1   https://www.gov.uk/government/news/pm-outlines-his-ten-point-plan
    -for-a-green-industrial-revolution-for-250000-jobs

2   https://ec.europa.eu/commission/presscorner/detail/en/IP_20_1599

the technologies that will be needed to reduce emissions: offshore wind, solar power, green hydrogen and electric vehicles. As this book is being written, Brussels is about to release its taxonomy of sustainable investments, a set of guidelines that are intended to define which technologies, and under which conditions, can be labelled as 'green'. The taxonomy is intended to make it easier to finance sustainable investments, by channelling public as well as private resources away from non-sustainable ventures.[3]

On the other side of the Atlantic, President Joe Biden promised to reverse ex-President Donald Trump's climate-sceptic agenda. Under Trump, the US pulled out of the Paris Agreement.[4] Under this accord, 189 countries[5] pledged to take appropriate measures to keep global temperature increases 'well below 2 °C', and possibly below 1.5 °C. The White House scaled down its support for renewable energies and introduced new subsidies for coal.[6] Instead, President Biden has put forward a plan for what is described as a clean energy revolution and programme for environmental justice,[7] under which the US also promises to achieve carbon neutrality by 2050. President Biden also committed

---

3 https://ec.europa.eu/info/business-economy-euro/banking-and-finance/sustainable-finance/eu-taxonomy-sustainable-activities_en

4 https://unfccc.int/process-and-meetings/the-paris-agreement/the-paris-agreement

5 https://unfccc.int/process-and-meetings/the-paris-agreement/the-paris-agreement

6 https://www.enerdata.net/publications/executive-briefing/biden-fight-against-global-warming.html

7 https://joebiden.com/climate-plan/

the US to a 50–52 per cent reduction in emissions by 2030 to below 2005 levels.[8]

China is promoting a 'green industrial revolution' too. Speaking before the United Nations in September 2020, President Xi Jinping pledged to achieve carbon neutrality by 2060.[9] This was seen as a major departure from Beijing's traditional stance on climate change: while recognising global warming as a major challenge and admitting that China should play its part, Chinese negotiators had, until then, argued that emerging economies in which carbon emissions per capita were below those in the developed world had a right to pursue economic growth even if that meant increased emissions. Xi's U-turn apparently relies on a plan developed by climate scientists at the Tsinghua University's Institute of Energy, Environment and Economy. Under the plan, coal would be phased out by 2050, while renewables and nuclear would take the place of fossil fuels in covering both the existing and additional energy demand.[10] In the meantime, new coal-fired power plants are being, and will be, installed in the country: in 2020 Beijing's total coal capacity rose by 29.8 GW, almost twice as much as the *cut* in coal capacity in the rest of the world (–17.2 GW).[11]

---

8   https://www.whitehouse.gov/briefing-room/statements-releases/2021/
    04/22/fact-sheet-president-biden-sets-2030-greenhouse-gas-pollution-re
    duction-target-aimed-at-creating-good-paying-union-jobs-and-securing
    -u-s-leadership-on-clean-energy-technologies/

9   https://www.bbc.com/news/science-environment-54256826

10 https://www.bloomberg.com/news/articles/2020-09-28/china-s-top
    -climate-scientists-lay-out-road-map-to-hit-2060-goal

11 https://www.reuters.com/article/us-china-coal-idUSKBN2A308U

If these promises are taken seriously, there are good reasons for optimism regarding carbon emissions. In 2019, the EU (including the UK), the US and China accounted for 9.4, 14.8 and 27.5 per cent of global CO_2 emissions, respectively. However, this still only represents around 50 per cent of all CO_2 emissions, so this optimism should not be unbounded. Furthermore, the UK is responsible for only 1 per cent of global CO_2 emissions. Decisions by individual countries or, indeed, regions only take us so far when it comes to reducing carbon emissions.

It is largely for this reason that there are international discussions and agreements relating to carbon emissions. Most recently, there was a Conference of the Parties (COP) meeting in Glasgow. This was the 26th such meeting (COP26). At the 21st meeting in Paris, 195 countries signed up to the Paris Agreement, which committed them to keep global temperatures 'well below' 2 °C above pre-industrial times and 'endeavour to limit' them to 1.5 °C. In addition, the industrialised countries agreed to pay US$100 billion a year by 2020 to help developing countries to decarbonise their economies.

At COP26, countries agreed plans to cut methane emissions and eliminate deforestation. They also agreed to phase out fossil fuel subsidies and 'phase down' the use of coal. In addition, 151 countries submitted plans for reductions in carbon emissions, but it is thought by the UN that these plans are only compatible with warming of 2.5 °C rather than the 1.5 °C aspiration. On a more optimistic note, the International Energy Agency claimed that, if the commitments made in Glasgow are met, the global temperature increase will only be of 1.8 °C by 2100.[12] At any rate, the COP26 agreement requires countries to revisit and strengthen their 2030 carbon reduction targets by the end of 2022.

Overall we have a situation where there is considerable global political coordination of policy. In addition, most countries have chosen a route to cutting carbon emissions that involves targets and governments picking specific technologies in the hope that their adoption will lead to their countries meeting their targets. There is a strong emphasis in communications on dressing up costs of emissions reductions (such as 'green jobs') as benefits. This approach, it can be said, leads to the maximum of headlines and, perhaps, hides the costs of reducing emissions.

While climate plans have been for some time at the heart of energy policy, things began to change in 2021 as the price of energy commodities soared to unprecedented levels, especially in Europe. National governments and the EU Commission suggested that high energy prices could fuel inflation, undermine economic growth and create social hardship if not unrest, since their impact is disproportionately high on those on low- and fixed-incomes. Governments reacted by pouring taxpayers' money into policies aimed at mitigating the increases of the prices of electricity, natural gas and oil products. When Russia invaded Ukraine, prices rose even further. As we write, the possibility of an oil and gas embargo is being seriously

---

12 https://www.iea.org/commentaries/cop26-climate-pledges-could-help -limit-global-warming-to-1-8-c-but-implementing-them-will-be-the-key

debated, which could put energy prices under even more stress. Energy inflation created some tension between the actual policy of keeping prices low and the stated objective of phasing out fossil fuels and promoting renewable energies. For example, several countries (such as Spain, Italy, France and Romania) introduced windfall profit taxes or various types of price caps (or both) on energy companies. The UK already has an energy price cap and is bringing in a form of windfall profits tax. Still, the long-run commitment to reduce the reliance on fossil fuels and to shift toward green energies became even stronger. The current situation may have induced governments to deviate from the decarbonisation path temporarily, but it also reinforced the claim that more (taxpayers') money should be invested in carbon-free sources of energy. In the long run, it is likely that both government and private investment will be channeled towards these sources of energy: hundreds of billions of pounds will be directed every year toward technologies that are picked by policymakers, even though they have not necessarily emerged as the most efficient solutions from market competition. Is it the best way to reduce emissions while achieving energy security?

Climate change: the economic context

Today the focus of the debate concerning energy policy seems to be energy security – and for good reasons. But before the invasion of Ukraine, and presumably at some stage in the future, it was (and will be again) climate change. Carbon neutrality is likely to remain the pillar of energy policy. And even the post-war policies are being designed in a way that aims at cutting emissions as soon and as radically as possible. This book is focused on how climate policy may be reformed so as to become aligned with the targets of economic efficiency, and not just environmental effectiveness. The quest for a sound and balanced policy was crucial before the war, because large sums of money and increasingly intrusive regulation were adopted under the flag of climate neutrality. Seeking economic efficiency, along with environmental sustainability, is even more important now that energy prices seem to have reached a new, higher baseline and that the expected rates of economic growth have been revised substantially downwards, while inflation is biting in a way not seen for decades. Therefore, understanding the reasons behind climate policy is now more urgent than ever – and it is the unavoidable precondition for moving from an interventionist climate agenda to a market-based approach.

The climate has always changed and yet, historically, natural changes in climate have not been regarded as an economic policy concern. What makes the process of global warming that we see today, and are likely to see in the future, different is that it arises directly from human activity and it is faster than at any time previously. The focus of economic policy is anthropogenic climate change in the form of global warming arising largely from carbon emissions – especially CO_2 and methane. In this short book, we take the position that this is a problem and one that will dwarf most natural changes in the climate that would be expected from decade to decade.

It does not necessarily follow that we should try to reduce carbon emissions to zero, still less try to reduce global warming to zero, even if that were possible. Indeed, it is worth pointing out in passing that there are some positive effects of global warming. Global warming will benefit some communities, especially in very cold parts of the world. In addition, some of the costs of global warming might be offset by benefits arising from increased vegetation growth caused by higher levels of carbon dioxide in the atmosphere.[13] More pertinently, however, when it comes to considering carbon-reduction policy, it should be noted that it might be possible to adapt to climate change more cheaply than we can reduce carbon emissions. Indeed, nobody suggests that we should take actions that would eliminate and reverse warming trends. As ever, in economics, there are trade-offs. The question that is widely discussed, therefore, is the extent to which we should try to reduce carbon emissions and global warming.

Related to this point, the costs of reducing carbon emissions may be greater than the costs of climate change, especially when we take into account the timeframe over which any benefits arising from policy action might take place and the likely improvement in our ability to adapt and mitigate the effects of climate change.

In this book, we make no judgement about the extent to which it is beneficial to reduce carbon emissions and try to reduce the trend of global warming. We merely highlight

13 https://climate.nasa.gov/news/2436/co2-is-making-earth-greenerfor-now/

that these issues cannot be ignored. They are widely debated in, for example, Stern (2007), Lomborg (2020) and Nordhaus (2018). Nordhaus (2018: 451) summarises the trade-off point effectively by noting in his Nobel Prize lecture:

> If, for example, attaining the 1.5°C goal would require deep reductions in living standards in poor nations, then the policy would be the equivalent of burning down the village to save it. If attaining the low-temperature path turns out to be easy, then of course we should aim for it.

Some argue that global warming is on a catastrophic trend. Those who are convinced that this is the case will believe that reducing global warming from current projected levels will bring large gains. However, additional, or marginal, gains from further reductions in global warming will fall as the projected level of warming reduces. At the same time, with current technology, the cost of reducing global warming rises as we try to reduce carbon emissions to a greater degree. It may be easy for countries to move to a situation whereby 50 per cent of their electricity is generated from renewable sources, but moving this figure to 100 per cent and then also replacing natural gas with renewable energy will be proportionately more expensive. There is a point at which further reductions in the trend of global warming are not worth the cost, unless new, better technologies become available (which may well happen at some point in the future).

Following Nordhaus's example, we can illustrate how this trade-off between the benefits and costs of reducing carbon emissions works by considering the position of the poor. It is often suggested that the poor suffer most from climate change. That might be true. However, that leaves open the question of the extent to which we should try to reduce carbon emissions bearing in mind that lower levels of economic growth and development that arise from reduced carbon emissions might prevent the poor from becoming richer and more resilient to extreme weather events. The adoption of air conditioning is a good example of this dilemma. A great deal of research has demonstrated huge reductions in excess deaths from heat through the use of air conditioning. This can be most effective in residential settings, but the benefits in hospitals are also enormous. But, there is a trade-off, as one research paper expressed it (Barreca et al. 2013):

> The similarity between the United States before 1960 and many developing countries today suggests that the greater use of air conditioning in these countries would significantly reduce mortality rates both today and in the future. Consequently, a primary finding of this paper is that the wider use of residential air conditioning should be near the top of the list of adaptation strategies in response to climate change–induced warming of the planet. At the same time, the greater use of residential air conditioning will speed up the rate of climate change ... It therefore seems that residential AC is both the most promising technology to help poor countries mitigate the temperature related mortality impacts of climate change and a technology whose proliferation will speed

up the rate of climate change. In many respects, this underscores the complicated nature of trying to mitigate the rate of climate change when any solution requires reductions in greenhouse gas emissions by countries with very different income levels.

Related to this point, it is interesting to look at trends in deaths from natural disasters.[14] Despite better reporting, they have fallen dramatically over time as the world has become richer and better able to adapt to problems. Deaths from natural disasters have fallen more than 90 per cent since the 1920s and by more than 75 per cent since the 1960s. This is despite big increases in the world population. Of course, if global warming occurs, it is likely that extreme weather events will increase. But, if there is a trade-off between economic development and reducing carbon emissions, it does not follow that there will be fewer deaths from those extreme weather events if we do more to reduce emissions. It is important that those who believe with conviction that climate change is happening and that we should therefore reduce carbon emissions address this point. Christian Aid recently released a report on property losses from natural disasters linking their occurrence strongly with climate change (Kramer and Ware 2021). Their conclusions were surprising because there was no time series analysis of losses and the warming of the climate: there was merely a set of case studies from a

---

14 The data in this paragraph is drawn from https://ourworldindata.org/natural-disasters.

particular year. As such, it was not possible to draw any causal links. In fact, global losses from natural disasters do not follow any particular pattern in the last 30 years and the number of recorded natural disasters has fallen.

None of this is intended to suggest that those who promote policies designed to reduce emissions are wrong. The fact that rising temperatures have not had much impact so far tells us little about the next 100 years. However, it is dangerous for politicians and campaign groups to use current data in relation to extreme weather events to justify their interventions just as it is dangerous for them to imply that reducing emissions has benefits rather than costs. Climate policy will lose credibility if its justifications are not sound.

The economics of climate change policy are made more difficult because the costs of climate change vary hugely between people and geographical areas. As noted above, some people might gain from climate change; on the other hand, others might lose greatly. Determining the net cost of global warming is impossible. We have seen the difficulty during the Covid crisis of applying scientific modelling to the progression of a disease and using such models to determine policy. Compared with measuring the impact of global warming, the parameters in the case of infectious diseases are several orders of magnitude simpler. Existing studies on the economic effects of climate change display a huge variability in estimates, ranging from 1–3 per cent to 5–10 per cent lower per capita GDP in 2100 (Kahn et al. 2019; Newell et al. 2021; Tol 2018). As economist John Cochrane has noted, the potential economic damage from climate change will be relatively small as compared with the expected GDP growth over the next few decades:

> Take even worst-case estimates that climate change will lower GDP by 5–10% in the year 2100. Compared to growth, that's couch change. At our current tragically low 2% per year, without even compounding (or in logs), GDP in 2100 will be 160% greater than now. Climate change will make 2100 be as terrible as ... 2095 would otherwise be.[15]

To be fair, there are substantial reasons to slow down climate change. Perhaps the most compelling one is that really serious effects from climate change are a low-probability, high-impact event that can be hardly captured by economic models (Wagner and Weitzman 2015). But basing the case for climate mitigation on unlikely scenarios – which may be sensible given what is at stake – also requires the design of climate policies in a way that minimises its (large and demonstrable) costs today, by avoiding inefficient or distortionary policies.

In addition, the net cost of global warming depends on the preferences that all individuals have in the world for different goods, services and for environmental conditions. There is simply no way of obtaining this information. We are therefore operating in a world of radical uncertainty. This makes any policy action highly contentious

---

15 https://johnhcochrane.blogspot.com/2021/07/how-much-does-climate-change-actually.html

for two reasons. Firstly, people have different views on how important it is to reduce projected global warming. Secondly, people will be affected by both the costs and benefits of policy action to different extents. People will therefore prioritise action in relation to global warming very differently.[16] Translating these economic preferences into political action is bound to be contentious. This may partly explain why politicians and campaign groups dress up the costs of climate change as benefits: in a public choice model, it helps motivate more people to support a policy.

World's biggest market failure?

Economists tend to think of global warming as an 'externality' arising from economic activity that emits greenhouse gases. In other words, costs are imposed on other people by those who emit carbon. The existence of this cost leads, in the economic jargon, to the marginal social cost of an economic activity involving the emission of greenhouse gases to be greater than the marginal private cost. We can also think of reductions in carbon emissions as a 'global public good' (Nordhaus 2018). If we reduce our emissions, at the level of an individual, family, locality or nation, we cannot exclude others from benefiting from

---

16 By way of analogy, even a project such as HS2 is highly contentious and this affects a relatively small number of communities. People differ hugely in their evaluations of its net benefits. In addition, different groups of people are affected, negatively or positively, to vastly different degrees by the project.

those reductions in emissions. This means that the price mechanism does not adequately deal with the problem.

Global warming was described, memorably, by Stern (2007) as the biggest market failure the world has ever seen. This is a tendentious description. We cannot define and trade property rights in an atmosphere containing a given level of carbon dioxide. Market participants cannot, therefore, benefit from their own actions in reducing carbon emissions or bear the costs of emissions. There is simply an absence of a market here – the market has not failed. Describing climate change as a market failure is like describing a car as a 'car failure' if it cannot sprout wings and fly. It is possible, it should be noted, for 'polycentric' solutions to emission reductions to develop as we note in the discussion below (chapter 5 and Ostrom 1990). In such approaches, there is action at many levels (individual, family, local government, within businesses, culturally, and so on). However, polycentric solutions are unlikely to be sufficient to meet government targets.

Can governments succeed where markets are said to fail?

If we cannot rely on markets to deal with the problem of climate change, the normal approach is to propose government action. But there are several problems here too. The first is that government policy is not a process that naturally leads to the most efficient outcome. Indeed, as a process, it might even lead to outcomes that cause more harm than good. We have mentioned above the impossibility of governments obtaining the information that is necessary to determine the 'optimal' degree to which we should reduce carbon emissions. Accumulating this information is not a technical problem to be solved – the relevant information does not exist.[17] Secondly, as the public choice literature shows, policy might be determined by interest groups of various types rather than by what is best for promoting economic welfare.[18] As we discuss below, we see this at work in current policy. Sometimes, this is described in the literature as 'government failure'. However, we think this term is as unhelpful as 'market failure'. The institutions of government simply cannot deliver optimal policy.

In addition, there is a collective action problem at the global level. The incentives for any one country (or group of countries in the case of the EU) to act is limited unless other countries act too. The benefits of actions to reduce carbon emissions taken by the UK are shared among the countries of the world as a whole and yet the costs are entirely born by citizens of the UK. Again, this is discussed by Nordhaus (2018). If this collective action problem is to be solved, it requires international agreements, such as COP26. However, international agreements are not a sufficient condition for incentivising countries to reduce carbon emissions because enforcement is difficult when there is no obvious sanction against countries that do not

---

17 Pennington (2021) discusses the 'information problem' in relation to choosing policy during the pandemic. The observation is essentially based on Hayekian reasoning. Pennington's article also addresses climate change policy.

18 A summary of the public choice literature is given in Butler (2012).

fall into line. Finally, the recognition of the existence of an externality or a public good raises a case for some form of collective action, but that does not mean that all policy tools are equally efficient, or that all policy goals are equally sound. Even more so, it does not imply that governments should engage in producing the public good or reducing the externality by themselves (Forte 1967).

Concluding comments

There will be disagreements among readers of this book about the extent to which action to deal with global warming is desirable. We make no comment on whether the chosen COP26 target is the right one. We will assume, for the sake of illustrating our arguments, that countries at the COP 26 conference have come to a reasonable decision to keep warming to 1.5 °C on the basis that they believe that the costs of reducing global warming are outweighed by the benefits up to that point. We will take this objective as given and examine the ways in which the policies designed to achieve it deviate significantly from those which most economists would recommend. There will be a particular focus on energy taxes and subsidies. Given that a policy decision has been taken to reduce carbon emissions and given the costs of reducing emissions, it is important that mechanisms are chosen that achieve the objective by the greatest amount for a given cost or that reduce emissions by a given amount at the lowest cost. This is not where policy is currently.

2   PROBLEMS OF CURRENT POLICY, AND ALTERNATIVE FRAMEWORKS

Seeking winners and picking losers

As can be seen from some of the rhetoric quoted at the beginning of chapter 1, green policies are normally promoted as providing benefits for the general economy. Phrases such as 'green jobs', 'green industrial revolution' and so on are used. However, the jobs that are 'created' as a result of green policies and the technologies in which capital is invested represent costs of limiting carbon emissions and climate change and not benefits. As public choice economics would suggest, politicians appear to want to hide the costs by describing them as benefits. This is problematic because, around the world, politicians seem to be choosing policies the costs of which are most easily hidden rather than policies that reduce emissions at minimum costs. Such an approach is both bad for the environment and bad for the economy. This mindset encourages a central planning approach and one that involves trying to 'pick winners' when it comes to green technologies. Politicians must accept that reducing emissions leads to costs and they should not dress costs up as benefits.

Most major countries, as noted above, have adopted similar approaches to reducing carbon emissions. This is despite the fact that different countries have different problems to deal with and are at different levels of development. The most efficient road to carbon neutrality depends on a number of variables, including GDP per capita, expected economic growth, place- and culture-specific variables, institutional design, the composition of the economy, the level of technology that has already been adopted and its current carbon-efficiency. How is it possible that countries with such diverse realities share the same recipe for decarbonisation? All of them seem to predicate their own green industrial revolution upon government intervention and the same choice of technologies, with just minor variations (for example, whether, and to what extent, to rely on nuclear power). Underlying this appearance is the common assumption that governments 'know' how to achieve emission reductions – so they just have to pick technologies, fund investments, and determine how energy systems shall change in the next few decades.

The central planning approach makes two errors. The first is that it is, as a matter of fact, impossible for governments to know in advance the best technologies for reducing carbon emissions, especially over a relatively long time span. The second is that it is based on the implicit assumption that the solution lies in the area of technology rather than, for example, energy conservation or measures to reduce consumption that individual consumers might choose to make. Such measures might arise from behavioural changes or from the adoption of technology.

However, which approach is most efficient and which technologies are appropriate will depend on the circumstances of particular households.

An approach to carbon reduction that involves subsidising particular technologies is both a cause of and a consequence of the process of political lobbying. Governments open up the policymaking process to special interests that benefit from promoting favoured technologies. Those special interests then drive policy. Organised interests spend a great deal of resources trying to convince policymakers of the appropriateness of specific solutions to decarbonisation: a process known as 'capture' (Stigler 1971; Laffont and Tirole 1991). For example, Helm (2008) argued:

> climate change ... is likely to be one of the largest sources of economic rents from policy interventions. There is a large and growing climate change 'pork-barrel'. It is highly unlikely that the policy costs will be zero. Indeed, there are good reasons to suppose otherwise – at every level of climate change policy.

Helm's prophecy was made in 2008 when governments all over the world were already pouring money into their preferred technologies to abate emissions. State interventionism in the energy sector was nothing new, of course. Taxes, subsidies, regulations and direct intervention through state-owned monopolies had been the norm for a century (Bradley 1996; Helm 2003). However, at the time governments were formulating policies in relation to climate change, several jurisdictions – including the UK, the EU,

21

and the US – had been pursuing a policy of market-opening in the energy industry. This was led by British reforms both privatising former monopolies and liberalising markets. The UK's success stimulated innovation elsewhere. For a short time, it was market forces, not political decisions, that mainly drove investments and technological switches in the energy sector. The policy environment caused by the desire for action in relation to climate change reversed this trend. This need not have been so.

Seeking to ban losers

Similar problems arise when governments decide to ban particular technologies. The UK government, for example, has committed itself to phasing out the sale of petrol and diesel cars and vans by 2030, while the EU is considering the same policy from 2035. Gas boilers are also to be phased out. Both of these technologies cause a substantial proportion of UK emissions. However, we argue below that a better climate change policy would involve taxing carbon emissions to the extent appropriate given the assumed social cost of carbon emissions. Individuals and businesses can then choose the cheapest ways to reduce their emissions. For many, this might involve keeping petrol-powered cars and making other sacrifices. Banning technologies presupposes that the government can predict the technological developments that are most likely to replace current everyday uses of carbon-intensive fuels. It may be the case that governments ban a technology that turns out extremely expensive to replace with a carbon-neutral alternative while another technology that is cheaper to replace is not prohibited. Once again, the government simply does not have the knowledge to make these decisions years, or even decades, in advance of alternative technologies becoming viable.

In addition, phasing out petrol cars and gas-fired boilers almost guarantees that there will be no commercial return from making them more carbon efficient in the future or low-carbon biofuels from developing. In addition, households are likely to bring forward from after the ban date the purchase of the banned items so that they are purchased just before the date they are phased out. This will reduce the impact of a policy that is, in any case, highly inefficient.

For some people, more efficient boilers or cars (such as hybrids or plug-in hybrids, depending on use patterns), combined with other behavioural adjustments, might be the cheapest way for them to reduce emissions. Given that gas-fired boilers and petrol cars will be used for many years after their purchase is phased out, the disincentive to invest in making them more efficient could undermine emission-reduction policies. These policies of banning particular types of technology are especially perverse in the case of household boilers given the decisions of governments to implicitly subsidise domestic natural gas consumption over several decades (see below). Banning technologies is a further way in which governments can hide the cost of reducing carbon emissions because, when alternatives are purchased, no cost comparison can be made with the banned product. Bans also provide a further vehicle for rent seeking by those hoping to gain from the replacement technologies having strong incentives to lobby for the prohibitions.

Other examples of illogical bans include the bans on hydraulic fracturing ('fracking') or nuclear power that have been considered or introduced by several EU member states. Shale gas might provide a low-carbon and nuclear power a carbon-free alternative to coal in power generation. By the same token, some countries have considered or introduced bans on carbon capture and sequestration. The jury is out regarding their economic viability, depending on time-, site- and technology-specific variables. However, though we might, in the future, observe *ex post* that a specific technology did not prove to be competitive enough, or well-performing enough, to gain market viability, this does not mean that we should dictate *ex ante* that it should be banned altogether. If these technologies are not, as their critics claim, economically sustainable, they will attract little investment in a competitive market, or investors will pay the price for their mistakes. But, if they are both economically and environmentally sound, a ban would just lead to the value that would have been created being forgone.

Taxes and subsidies

A second aspect of current policy is an array of taxes and subsidies that are purportedly designed to reduce carbon emissions but which, in fact, are irrational and promote rent-seeking. This will be discussed in further detail in the next chapter.

According to a study sponsored by the EU Commission (EC 2020a–c), from 2008 to 2018, total energy subsidies in the EU27 (excluding the UK) increased by 67 per cent in real terms, from €95 billion to €159 billion annually.[1] In 2019 and 2020 the amount of subsidies further increased to €176 and €177 billion, respectively (EC 2021). This includes subsidies to energy sources that emit greenhouse gases. Strangely, governments simultaneously subsidise and tax the same forms of energy. The revenue from taxes on energy consumption in the EU27 was €263 billion in 2018.

Energy production, transformation and consumption are major sources of externalities, including climate change and local pollution. External costs from energy use were estimated by the EU Commission to be €340.6 billion in the EU27 and €30.4 billion in the UK in 2018.

As the following chapters will show, despite the voluminous economic literature on optimal taxation and the management of externalities, there is no relationship between taxes, subsidies and external costs from energy use in the UK or the EU. Taxes are generally used to raise revenue rather than to align the private and social costs of energy. Subsidies, although ostensibly designed to help decarbonise the economy, appear to reflect the ability of rent seekers to capture the political process. As a result, the same fuel is taxed differently depending on the context in which it is used. In addition, different clean energies are

---

1   Throughout this book, data about energy taxes and subsidies in the UK and the EU, unless otherwise specified, are from the database underlying the EU Commission–sponsored study on 'Energy prices and costs in Europe' (see EC 2020a–c).

awarded different subsidies despite having similar benefits, and some fossil fuels are either taxed or subsidised or sometimes both taxed and subsidised in different contexts. Neither taxes nor subsidies can be reconciled with the ultimate goal of fiscal interventions in welfare economics: making the polluters pay and pursuing decarbonisation efficiently.

If policy in relation to taxes and subsidies is unrelated to economic consequences, then any given reduction in carbon emissions will come at a greater economic cost. However, given the cost of reducing emissions, it is especially important they are reduced at the lowest feasible economic cost. The more ambitious are the targets, the more important this is. Climate change is too important a problem to be addressed in such a disordered and irrational way. An economically rational climate change strategy should aim to reduce carbon emissions at minimum cost. It should not consist of badly designed taxes and subsidies with the economic rents handed out to interest groups.

Coase or Pigou?

Intuitively, there should be a relationship between taxes, subsidies and external costs that given activities impose on others. Externalities in this case are costs imposed on third parties and not fully captured by market prices. Many economists, citing Pigou (1932), argue that goods that produce such negative externalities should be taxed in order to align the private costs of products and their market price with their social costs (including impacts on third parties). There is an alternative. In many cases, clearer definitions of property rights can help bring about efficient solutions to environmental problems so that market prices reflect the environmental and other costs from human action (Coase 1960, 1974). Coasean approaches to environmental problems can be regarded as superior because they are better able to reflect preferences for environmental harms and goods as is indicated in the following example.

Imagine a factory close to a housing development where all the houses are owned by the same institution and let to tenants. Assume that the factory makes a noise and that this causes harm to the residents and, as a result, they will only live on the development at lower rents than they would have done without the noise. As long as the law defines clearly whether those in the houses have a right to a quiet environment or, alternatively, that they have no right and the factory has a right to make a noise, there is a potential for an efficient solution. If the house owners have a legal right for their tenants not to be affected by noise, the factory could compensate the development owner for the right to make a noise. If that sum were greater than the reduction in rents received arising from the impact of the noise, the development owner would accept the sum. A sufficient sum may be offered if the value to the factory from making the noise were high. This might be because of the cost of making changes to the industrial processes or because of the cost to the factory owner of moving the factory away. Alternatively, if the development owner does

27

not have a right to a quiet life, he could pay the factory owner to eliminate the noise. If the value of a quiet life to the tenants, as reflected by the rent differential, is greater than the value to the factory owner of being able to make the noise, the factory owner will accept the payment and eliminate the noise.

Such approaches can be highly efficient. This example has been constructed as if there is a binary variable – noise or no noise. But negotiation could lead to some reduction in noise for a smaller payment. The solution would depend on exactly how much those living on the development valued a quiet life and how valuable it was to the manufacturer to make different levels of noise. These preferences can be revealed in the actions of the tenants, developer owner and factory owner. Behaviours can then be adapted in sophisticated ways.

Unfortunately, the application of Coasean approaches relies on 'transactions costs' being sufficiently low to make them viable. These transactions costs include the costs of bargaining, contracting, enforcing contracts and defining the property rights. It is impossible to imagine such an approach being taken with climate change, where the emissions of the whole world impact to a differing degree on the people of the whole world and display their effects over several decades.

The Pigovian alternative involves taxes being levied to reflect the damage caused to one party by the activities of another (Pigou 1932). There can be some further complexities but, in simple terms, the tax should be levied at a rate that reflects the difference between the private costs of activities that lead to greenhouse gas emissions and the social costs (including the costs of global warming). The social costs are those costs borne by non-contracting parties. The private cost of making steel will be paid by the purchaser of steel. However, if making steel imposes costs on others through carbon emissions, these are additional costs not captured in the price of steel.

As noted above, it is impossible to determine the social costs in practice and the costs will vary between communities with some people benefiting from global warming. Thus, when we use taxes to try to reflect externalities, we are groping in the dark trying to estimate some measure of aggregate social cost. Because of this, Coasean solutions should be used where feasible but, in the case of global warming, they are not.

Nevertheless, two things are clear from economic reasoning. The first is that subsidies for carbon-emitting fuels cannot be justified. As is mentioned above, COP26 led to a commitment to phase such subsidies out, but there have been other such commitments with little action. Secondly, although the problem of estimating the externalities from carbon emissions remain, the use of taxes on carbon emissions does, at least, ensure that people will be incentivised to reduce emissions in ways that have the lowest cost. Current policy, by which governments promote particular technologies to try to reduce carbon emissions, is inefficient because there is no effective market information on the costs and benefits of the methods used. On the other hand, a tax on carbon emissions allows individuals to use the information about the costs and benefits of different economic activities so that they can find the lowest-cost approaches to reducing emissions. This may involve reducing carbon-intensive activities (such as driving less or reducing meat intake), the use of new technologies or energy conservation in the home which can, in turn, come about in several ways (for example, accepting domestic heating at lower temperatures or in fewer rooms or via improved insulation).

Carbon trading, Coase or Pigou?

An alternative to taxing carbon emissions is to use carbon trading schemes. Here, the total level of emissions is capped and emitters have to purchase carbon credits if they wish to increase their emissions. Such schemes can work quite well, especially as there can be a very direct focus on the total amount of emissions that are allowed each year. When taxes are levied to reduce emissions, the extent to which reductions will be achieved will depend on the supply and demand response to the imposition of the tax. This cannot be known in advance.

Cap-and-trade schemes are sometimes regarded as 'Coasean' because they establish a form of property right in carbon emissions. This analogy is drawn in the otherwise excellent paper by Heal and Schlenker (2019).[2] This is

---

2 Heal and Schlenker's paper is quite technical, but it discusses various pros and cons of carbon taxes and emissions trading. It notes, correctly, that, under a carbon tax, fossil fuels would still be used and their use might stretch out longer into the future. This does not matter, however, as long as emissions are reduced sufficiently.

a false analogy, however. A cap-and-trade scheme takes no account of the extent to which people prefer climate change (with all the associated costs) or prefer emissions reductions (with all the costs involved in that process). The cap on emissions is set by government under the assumption that the government knows the necessary reduction in emissions that will achieve what it regards as the optimal amount of warming.

Taxes that reflect the externalities from carbon emissions and cap and trade are similar instruments. When taxes are used, the government sets the tax (a price) in the expectation of supply and demand adjusting to the desired level of emissions. If the tax does not achieve the desired effect because the government does not estimate its impact on demand and supply correctly, it can be increased or reduced. In a cap-and-trade scheme, the government sets the desired level of emissions directly and then the price is established in the market in which the rights to emit are traded. It can be shown that, under ideal conditions, the optimal tax would lead to a reduction in emissions equal to the optimal cap under a cap-and-trade scheme. Of course, ideal conditions are mere abstractions; hence there are practical reasons to prefer one instrument to the other.

The authors prefer a Pigovian tax to cap and trade. In the latter approach, lobbying can strongly influence the initial allocation of rights to emit carbon. Once those rights are allocated, if estimates of the cost of global warming reduce, the holders of rights to emit might resist the creation of further rights because it will cause the value of existing allocations to fall. As such, adjustment can be harder. The distributional effects of cap-and-trade schemes can also be complex and difficult to determine. With a Pigovian tax, the polluter pays. This would seem to us to be appropriate. As we will discuss later, if the tax hits the poor to too great an extent, other taxes can be reduced to compensate for this while still ensuring that producers and consumers pay the tax at the point at which they take decisions to emit or purchase products that lead to emissions. In addition, carbon taxes would be relatively easy to administer. We believe that, by making the costs of reducing emissions transparent, the political debate about global warming would take place in a climate conducive to better decision-making.

Moreover, a carbon tax is more clearly visible. This explains why carbon taxes may be politically more difficult to introduce. A cap-and-trade scheme is not directly perceived by consumers, who may support too strict a target under the false perception that 'big companies', not 'poor consumers', will eventually bear the costs.

Despite the reasons to prefer a carbon tax over a cap-and-trade scheme, the authors also believe that either a carbon tax or a cap-and-trade scheme are better and less distortionary than discretionary subsidies to low-carbon or carbon-free energy technologies. The main difference between a tax and a cap-and-trade mechanism lies in the greater transparency of the former. But both are much more transparent than alternative instruments whereby policymakers crowd out any form of competitive selection by picking the preferred technologies top-down.

We have already considered how current policy is highly inefficient and possibly counter-productive. We prefer pricing instruments to the subsidisation of some and the prohibition of other technologies. But, even when governments use pricing to reduce carbon emissions, they do it badly, often trying to hide costs of adaptation by subsidising alternatives to carbon-intensive fuels. Overall, there is a chaotic regime of taxes and subsidies in place. In the following chapters, we examine this in more detail and propose an alternative.

Concluding comments

In the last few years there has been a huge increase in intervention in energy markets. This is particularly marked in the UK where there had been, in the 1990s, significant liberalisation. The policies described above and in the following chapters are just a snapshot of a labyrinthine set of interventions which are incoherent and have often had the opposite of their intended effect. Indeed, at the time of writing, the UK market is suffering the effects of price control. In 2021, rising gas prices led to increased power prices all over Europe and in the UK, with wholesale power prices rising by 50 per cent or more. In Great Britain the government has imposed a price cap on retail prices. This prevented price increases from being passed on to final consumers immediately. Partly as a result of this, a large number of the active power retailers stopped supplying because of their failure to anticipate high energy prices combined with the effect of price caps. This left approximately two million customers dependent on the suppliers of last-resort designed by the regulator Ofgem. Much of the political response to this has involved proposals for subsidies at the very time when governments around the world are signing up to agreements to reduce emissions.

The remainder of this book examines in more detail the inefficiency of current policy in terms of its chaotic array of taxes and subsidies. We then consider how we might abolish subsidies and levy a straightforward carbon tax.

3 ENERGY TAXES AND SUBSIDIES: WHY THEY EXIST IN THEORY AND IN PRACTICE

The chaotic nature of energy taxes

As discussed above, economists consider energy taxes to be an instrument that can be used to ensure that a polluter pays the difference between the marginal private and the marginal social cost of a particular activity following the work of Arthur C. Pigou (see Mirrlees 2011; Pigou 1932). In the case of carbon emissions, the social cost over and above private costs arises principally from the damage caused by global warming. There are other social costs too, such as the emission of particulates in cities. In practice, as discussed later, it might be appropriate to deal with such different forms of social cost in different ways.

Historically, energy taxes have been implemented to raise revenues for the government. Energy demand is relatively price inelastic, especially in the short run, although evidence suggests that it becomes more elastic as technological progress provides consumers with alternative fuels and devices (Andersson 2019). As such, energy sources can provide a reliable and relatively stable tax base. This has made taxes on certain types of energy use attractive to governments.

Whatever their origins and purposes, if taxes are levied on energy they result in higher prices. Hence, they change the relative prices of technologies, energy sources and uses in a way that depends on the design of the taxes. Taxes will influence both demand for and supply of different energy sources. They can ensure that the polluters pay for the environmental damage they cause even if the purpose of the tax is not to rectify the environmental damage. However, given the way that taxes on fuel have developed, there is no guarantee that the pattern of taxes adopted in practice will reflect externalities. If taxes are not levied in proportion to the externality arising from the use of a particular fuel, they will distort markets and may not even bring social and private costs closer together.

Indeed, it is the case that the relationship between environmental damage (or other externalities) and energy taxation is weak in most countries – certainly in the UK. The same energy source is often taxed differently depending on how it is used even though the social costs arising from, for example, carbon emissions will not depend on how the energy source is used. For example, in nearly every country, burning kerosene in an aeroplane attracts no tax (see Seely 2019), but burning closely related diesel in a car attracts excise duties in the UK and the equivalent in most other countries. Farmers do not pay tax on diesel they burn even though other businesses and individuals do. This both distorts the transport market and, in so far as modes of transport compete, will reduce the impact of taxing diesel on overall carbon emissions. To give another example, in some countries, natural gas used for business purposes is taxed more than natural gas used for heating homes. This means that businesses may bear the costs of externalities arising from carbon emissions, but house-holders may not do so. In turn, this means that businesses will have incentives to reduce carbon emissions which are absent in the case of households. This means that businesses may spend money on reducing emissions when it would be much cheaper for households to do so. It is also worth noting, given trends during the Covid pandemic, that businesses operating from a residence will not pay value added tax on fuel whereas businesses working from specific business premises will do so.

Because of this chaotic system of taxes, countries do not use efficient ways of reducing carbon emissions. Fur-thermore, it is clear that interest groups are at work in determining policy in relation to energy taxes.

The chaotic nature of energy subsidies

The pattern of subsidies tells a similar story. In principle, an economic case can be made for subsidies if they sup-port technologies or behaviours that result in positive externalities. For example, it is argued that subsidies for research and development into clean(er) energies are an important component of any meaningful climate strategy (Acemoglu et al. 2012; Sung 2019). Innovation can produce positive externalities – it results in larger benefits than those captured by the innovators alone; and, in addition, it is argued that subsidising research in this field is justified given the urgency of the problem of climate change.

This perspective on the value of government subsidies for research and innovation is disputed (see Kealey and Ricketts 2014; Kealey 2021). But, even if the externality argument were valid, only a small proportion of total subsidies in the energy sector are directed towards research, development and innovation. In 2018, only 2.9 per cent of total energy subsidies were directed towards such activities in the EU.

The largest share of energy subsidies support energy production (53.3 per cent in the EU) or consumption (32.5 per cent in the EU). These subsidies apply to both fossil fuels and renewable energies. This leads to the question of whether there is some kind of positive externality that justifies such fiscal transfers. This is difficult to argue. In the case of fossil fuels, subsidies not only lack justification, they are highly likely to increase environmental harm (Coady et al. 2019).[1]

The most significant subsidy in the UK arises from the exemption of domestic fuel from the full rate of value added tax (VAT). Why is exemption from VAT a subsidy?[2] VAT is intended to be a general tax on consumption. In essence, it is a proportional tax on income less saving (or

---

1   In theory, there are some circumstances in which environmental harms will not be increased. It is possible to suggest exceptional cases in which, for example, the demand for energy overall is highly inelastic, but there is a high cross-price elasticity between fuels. In this case, a subsidy to the fuel associated with the lowest emissions while that associated with the highest emissions remains unsubsidised might reduce overall emissions. However, the best policy would be a tax on both fuels, but a higher tax on the higher-emitting one. See further discussion below.

2   Or, as it is sometimes described, a 'tax expenditure'.

income plus dis-saving). An exemption from VAT for an energy source reduces its relative price as compared with that of other goods in the same way that a subsidy would. In general, therefore, tax exemptions, or tax expenditures, are regarded by economists in the same way as subsidies. The charging of a lower rate of VAT on domestic fuel consumption is a major fuel subsidy in the UK.

There is little empirical work on the impact of UK fossil fuel subsidies on carbon emissions. However, research in the Republic of Ireland suggests that the removal of fossil fuel subsidies in all sectors other than agriculture would lead to a 20 per cent fall in carbon emissions in Ireland between 2020 and 2030. The impact of their removal in the UK would be different, partly because subsidies per head in Ireland are approximately twice the level of those in the UK, but also they have a different profile. However, this figure gives some indication of their effect.

The experience of the UK in this area demonstrates the problems caused by interest groups influencing policy. In 1993, the Conservative government proposed charging VAT at the full rate, then 17.5 per cent, on domestic fuel. A rate of 8 per cent was to be charged from April 1994 and 17.5 per cent from 1995. When it was announced, the measure was justified both by fiscal necessity and by carbon reduction targets. In December 1994, the government was defeated in a vote in the House of Commons and the rate was held at 8 per cent.

The Labour Party had strongly opposed the removal of this subsidy. In the following election, in 1997, the Labour Party had relatively few specific promises, but one of them was to lower the rate of VAT on domestic fuel to 5 per cent. This was the lowest rate allowed at that time by EU rules. Interestingly, the 1997 Labour Party manifesto, in the paragraph immediately following the proposal to reduce VAT on domestic fuel, stated:

> Taxation is not neutral in the way it raises revenue. How and what governments tax sends clear signals about the economic activities they believe should be encouraged or discouraged, and the values they wish to entrench in society. Just as, for example, work should be encouraged through the tax system, environmental pollution should be discouraged.

This inconsistency demonstrates the difficulty of implementing policy in this area that is rational from an economic welfare perspective.

Renewable energies are the largest recipients of energy subsidies in today's developed world. These may seem easier to justify. But even subsidising renewable energies is unlikely to be the optimal policy. Renewable energies do not generate positive externalities – they simply lack the negative externalities that non-renewable fuels produce.[3]

---

3   For the sake of this discussion, we are ignoring non-carbon-related externalities. These can arise from both renewables and non-renewables. Such externalities include the risk of nuclear accidents or visual or environmental harms that arise from the construction of wind turbines. We are also ignoring the negative externalities that intermittent energy sources, such as wind and solar power, may cause to the power grid, thereby causing hidden costs to consumers (Borenstein 2012; Stagnaro 2015). Whether these are externalities is contestable as it could be suggested that these externalities

Renewables do not harm the climate: but this is not a positive externality.

The argument is often made that, if renewables are subsidised, their consumption will increase at the expense of the consumption of non-renewables. But whether this happens in practice depends on the price and income sensitivity of energy consumption and the relationship between the demand and supply functions for different types of energy. If renewables are subsidised, it is likely, though not certain, that their consumption would rise. It is probable that the consumption of carbon-intensive fuels would fall somewhat. But the extent to which carbon emissions will fall as a result of subsidising renewables is questionable. Such an approach also leaves untaxed the externality from carbon-intensive fuels.

The impact of renewable subsidies on carbon emissions may be limited for several reasons. Subsidising renewables may lead households to consume more energy overall, even if the energy mix is more weighted towards renewables. Households then have less of an incentive to invest in measures that will reduce energy consumption. In a similar way, subsidies for green transport might simply raise the demand for the transport in general while doing little to reduce demand for carbon-intensive methods of transport. Overall, subsidising renewables is a highly inefficient way to reduce emissions. However, because it hides the costs, it can be an approach that is very attractive to politicians.

---

are contained within the market. Nevertheless, it is very difficult to make the case that there are positive externalities from solar power, wind power, tidal energy and geothermal energy

The other problem with trying to reduce carbon emissions by using a complex web of varying subsidies is that it can lead to a further range of policies being developed to deal with the unintended consequences of the renewable energy subsidies. Such policies invite lobbying and rent-seeking and so may have a huge cost in overall terms. One example of the dangers of this approach is the combination of taxes and subsidies designed to promote the use of electric vehicles in Norway, which is regarded as a very-high-cost way of reducing emissions (see Skonhoft and Holtsmark 2014; Olsen 2015). Of course, the existence of subsidies for non-renewable fuels is likely to lead to pressure to subsidise renewables thus creating an institutional framework that is even more prone to lobbying from interest groups.

The first priority for policy reform should be the removal of subsidies on fossil fuels, following COP26 and earlier commitments: this is a clear win–win policy. But we would argue that subsidies on renewables should be removed as well.

Even if an economic case, based on environmental externalities, could be made for subsidies for renewable energy, it is clear that this is not the basis upon which subsidies are determined. The level of subsidy varies dramatically between renewable sources. For example, the average subsidy for solar power in 2018 was €248 per MWh in the EU. This was almost twice as high as that for offshore wind (€138 per MWh) and slightly less than five times as much as that for onshore wind (€54 per MWh). This suggests that policymakers view solar power as somehow 'better' renewable energy than wind power. If subsidies are to be used at all, an efficient approach would relate them to the reduction in emissions.

The cost of cutting carbon emissions depends on the specific situations in which an emitter finds themselves. However, the cost of replacing carbon-intensive fuels with renewables at these levels of subsidy is far greater than the actual cost of cutting emissions in the most efficient ways. The average cost of carbon permits in the European Emissions Trading System, of which the UK was also part at this time, was around €15.50 per tonne of CO_2 in 2018.[4] This suggests that businesses were willing to pay, at the margin, €15.50 to emit an extra tonne of carbon. In turn, those that sell carbon permits were willing to cut their carbon emissions by one tonne in return for €15.50. Electricity generated using natural gas produces about 0.4 tonnes of carbon per MWh.[5] The subsidy to renewables is significantly greater than the price of the carbon emitted by gas-generated electricity. An example of the importance of this point is that it may be the case that the most efficient way of reducing carbon emissions is to eliminate coal-generated electricity. Coal generation of electricity emits about twice as much carbon as gas generation.[6] The price of carbon permits to allow a generator to produce a MWh

---

4 https://www.eea.europa.eu/themes/climate/trends-and-projections -in-europe/trends-and-projections-in-europe-2019/the-eu-emissions -trading-system

5 https://www.parliament.uk/globalassets/documents/post/postpn_383 -carbon-footprint-electricity-generation.pdf

6 Ibid.

of coal-generated electricity is still way below the subsidy to renewables. This is true even as this paper is being written, in 2021, with soaring carbon prices at or above €50 per tonne of CO_2.

Whenever an energy source or technology is subsidised, the cost is borne either by taxpayers in general or by energy consumers in those situations where subsidies are financed by levies on energy bills. If the subsidy is greater than the expected positive externality, then society overpays for the energy source while consumers pay too little. Even more importantly, when taxpayers subsidise renewables in arbitrary ways, investment is no longer driven by the relative cost-effectiveness of different ways of cutting emissions but by the level of subsidies. As well as leading to inefficient ways of reducing carbon emissions, subsidising energy sources such as renewables creates an incentive for firms to invest in rent-seeking activities to obtain greater subsidies, rather than in research and development. Environmental lobbyists, campaign groups and charities (many of which may genuinely seek lower carbon emissions) also encourage such rent seeking because it helps promote their cause if the costs of a transition to a low-carbon economy are hidden.

Subsidising renewables increases the cost of reducing carbon emissions. An efficient climate policy, should reconcile energy taxes, subsidies and external costs in order to let the market (i.e. producers driven by consumer preferences) not the state (i.e. politicians driven by both their perception of the public good as well as by interest groups) take resource-allocation decisions.

4 ENERGY TAXES AND SUBSIDIES IN THE UK AND EUROPE

Energy taxes

In 2018, environmental taxes raised €324.6 billion in the EU27 and €56.7 billion (£47.6 billion)[1] in the UK, equal to 2.4 per cent and 2.3 per cent of GDP respectively. Of these, the largest chunk came from energy taxes. They generate revenue equal to 1.9 per cent and 1.7 per cent of EU and UK GDP respectively. About half of all energy taxation comes from transport fuel taxes, particularly excise taxes. They raised about 1.2 per cent of both EU and UK GDP (EC 2020d).

Energy taxes are not related to the externalities involved in the production and consumption of fuel. They vary according to the users of fuel and the uses to which fuel is put. The main rationale behind the current distribution of energy taxes seems to be the relative inelasticity of energy demand and supply together with the influence

---

1   Throughout, amounts will generally be quoted in euros for consistency of comparison between the UK and EU27 and because of the data sources used. The sterling figure here is at the exchange rate on 1 January 2021. At an average 2018 exchange rate, the sterling figure would be about 5 per cent lower.

of lobbyists. Governments seem to act as revenue- and vote-maximisers, not environmental-damage-minimisers, when they introduce a new tax or set its amount.

In principle, energy taxes can be levied upon energy production, consumption or on infrastructure. In practice, the burden of taxes will tend to fall upon consumers. Indeed, when we are imposing Pigovian taxes related to the externalities arising from energy sources, it is desirable that the incidence of the tax falls on consumers. It is their consumption choices that will, eventually, drive investment and commercial offers from suppliers in various markets.

There are several ways of classifying energy taxation. As noted above, we can classify taxes according to how energy is used (for example, farmers pay different energy taxes from delivery drivers). We can also classify them according to who uses the energy source: for example, several studies have shown that, in most EU member states, as well as in the UK, residential customers and SMEs pay a larger share of energy taxes than large businesses[2] (Trinomics 2020; CEPS and Ecofys 2018; Molocchi 2017). Finally, we can also classify them according to the source of energy (for example, natural gas, coal and so on). The Pigovian ideal would be to set taxes according to the level of externalities arising from the energy source. Who used the source and for what purpose it is used should be irrelevant.

---

2   Though, again, there are variations by energy use. This is more likely to be true for energy taxes related to transport than for energy taxes related to heating.

In order to understand how a tax modifies the behaviour of economic agents in the face of negative externalities, and to what extent it achieves the result of internalising external costs, there are limitations of using data at the aggregate level. Ideally, we would need to know data either for tax per unit of energy, where the level of emissions is the same per unit of energy used in different uses, or the tax per unit of emissions. Unfortunately, detailed data on the effective tax rates per unit of carbon emissions or, indeed, per unit of energy source are not available. This makes economic analysis of whether taxes are on average at about the right level extremely difficult and we have to make some approximations.

Here we approximate the taxation level for each energy source by averaging across uses and users. The same approach has been taken below for energy subsidies. Eurostat provides us with an estimate of energy taxes as well as the share attributable to fuel taxes which is largely accounted for by oil products. Fuel taxes, such as excise taxes or other duties on fuels for road transport and heating, account, on average, for 72 per cent of the revenues from energy taxes in the EU27+UK. The UK stands slightly below the average, with about 69 per cent of energy taxes arising from fuel taxes. The remaining share has been attributed to other energy sources (natural gas, nuclear and renewable energies) proportionally to energy consumption. A slight correction has been made to take into account that coal and natural gas pay larger taxes than carbon-free energy sources, both via the EU cap-and-trade schemes and via ad hoc excise taxes. As far as the EU27 is concerned, the median effective tax rates on natural gas and coal are €2 per MWh and €1 per MWh, respectively, while the median effective tax rate on electricity is €4 per MWh. However, the tax rates on gasoline and diesel are €59 per MWh and €37 per MWh respectively (see figure 1).

Figure 1   **Box plots of reported tax rates for key fuels,
by EU member state in 2018 (€/MWh)**

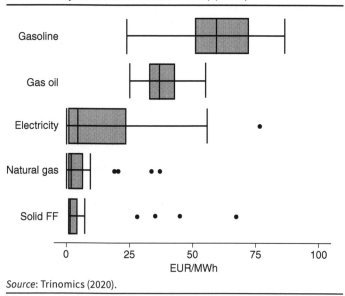

Source: Trinomics (2020).

As figure 1 shows, there is considerable variation in tax rates across EU member states. The line within the box shows the median tax rate and the edges of the box the quartiles. The far-right whisker on each box is 1.5 times greater than the 75th percentile and the far-left whisker is 1.5 times less than the 25th percentile. Dots represent outliers.

Based on these figures, the average tax burden has been estimated for each unit of energy which is consumed in the EU27 and the UK, by energy source. The calculation is made for gross inland consumption, i.e. the amount of energy gross of transformation and transport losses.

Figure 2   Taxes on energy sources in the UK and the EU27 (2018)

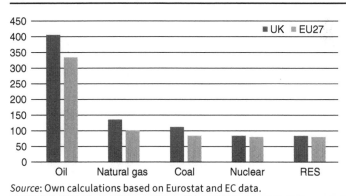

Source: Own calculations based on Eurostat and EC data.

It turns out that oil products are heavily taxed, both in the EU27 and the UK. Natural gas and coal bear much lower tax (about one quarter of the level of oil products). This difference is mainly due to excise taxes and other levies either on fuel itself or on its transformed output (for example, electricity). Nuclear and renewable energies are not subject to specific taxes so they are subject to the same taxes and levies that fall upon their transformed output, which is electricity. This is summarised in figure 2, where taxes are presented as the tax per tonne of oil equivalent

(TOE), i.e. the tax that would be borne by an amount of the energy source equivalent to the same amount of energy as a tonne of oil.

Energy taxes in the UK are somewhat higher than taxes in the EU27 for each type of fuel. Oil products are taxed on average at €405 per TOE in the UK compared with €334 per TOE in the EU27. Natural gas is taxed at €135 per TOE in the UK and €101 per TOE in the EU. Coal is taxed at €112 per TOE in the UK and €84 per TOE in the EU; and nuclear and renewables bear roughly the same tax of €84 per TOE in the UK and €80 per TOE in the EU.

Within the EU27 there is considerable variation in taxes. For example, oil products (such as gasoline and diesel) are taxed as little as €179 per TOE in Cyprus and as much as €487 per TOE in Italy. The variation is even larger for natural gas and electricity as these are subject to negligible taxes in some member states (particularly in countries in Central and Eastern Europe, such as Hungary, the Czech Republic and Poland) whereas there are significant taxes in other countries (such as in Denmark).

This variation is not, per se, a problem: each country should run the kind of fiscal policy that matches best the social preferences of its voters. What really matters, from the perspective of energy and environmental policy, is, firstly, whether environmental taxes are high enough to offset the external costs; secondly, how taxes change the *relative* prices of different energy sources; thirdly, how taxes change the price of energy relative to other goods and services. Taxing energy sources differently will affect the demand for each source. If tax-induced changes in relative prices do not reflect the external costs of each energy source, consumers are incentivised to demand more of an environmentally harmful, or otherwise costly, source of energy. From the standpoint of economic efficiency, tax policy should take this into account in order to follow the polluter pays principle. For example, taxing oil more than coal does not reflect this principle.

It should be emphasised that most energy taxes – including fuel taxes, excise taxes and other levies – fall upon the final consumer. That does not necessarily mean that the final consumer bears all (or even most) of the cost of the tax itself. The literature on tax incidence has extensively studied this phenomenon, showing that who actually pays the tax depends on a number of variables, most notably the relative price-elasticity of supply and demand. Given the low elasticity of energy demand, especially in the short run, most of the tax is passed through to consumers (Ganapati et al. 2020).

Energy taxes are only part of the story, though. In order to assess how, and to what extent, the fiscal system distorts the demand for and supply of energy sources we should also look at energy subsidies.

Energy subsidies

Like taxes, energy subsidies can take many forms. They may differ according to the use to which energy is put, providers of energy, types of energy, consumers of energy and the sectors in which energy is used. Choices regarding each of these dimensions may affect the extent of behavioural responses to price changes, the subsidy's incidence and its broader environmental effects.

By way of example, subsidies may apply to a given fuel for the whole economy or they may be targeted at specific economic sectors, such as households or small and medium enterprises. Subsidies may be designed as direct transfers, tax expenditures (i.e. a relief from normal taxes) or income or price supports for businesses. Another important distinction, though, is that between production and consumption subsidies. A high proportion of subsidies for renewables are production subsidies. Depending on the pattern of supply and demand and the competitive situation in the market, production subsidies could benefit producers rather than consumers. Subsidies to renewable electricity sources may result in a reduction in wholesale electricity prices and in consumer prices, at least in the hours when renewable energy is injected into the power grid (Bushnell and Novan 2018; Johnson and Oliver 2019). But this can be a small effect compared with the size of the subsidy.

Because the landscape is so complex, it is worth describing some of the specific subsidies that exist by way of example. There are also further examples listed in table 1. In the UK, VAT is charged at 5 per cent on domestic fuel consumption. This is below the standard rate of 20 per cent and is therefore a tax expenditure – a subsidy in effect. However, this subsidy only applies to households and not businesses. In Italy, the standard excise rate on diesel of €0.617 per litre and the VAT rate is 22 per cent. However, the excise duty rate is reduced to €0.136 per litre and the VAT rate to 10 per cent for farmers. In Germany, the feed-in tariff for small solar installations (i.e. a direct transfer to solar generators proportional to the amount of energy they produce) varies between 8.91 and 12.70 cents depending on where the panel is installed (for example, on roofs, facades or as noise barriers).

In the EU27 energy subsidies amounted to about €159 billion in 2018. Of these, slightly more than half (€85 billion) supported energy production. These were mainly subsidies for renewable production and increased from €37 billion in 2008. Subsidies of €52 billion were aimed at energy consumption. Subsidies to promote energy efficiency amounted to just €15 billion in 2018. There were smaller subsidies for the provision of energy infrastructure and research and development. The most subsidised form of energy was electricity (€108 billion). Subsidies to fossil fuels mostly took the form of tax expenditures or other forms of demand support, whereas subsidies to renewable energies were mostly designed as direct transfers or price supports to energy producers. The greatest direct beneficiaries from subsidies were energy producers (€92 billion in 2018, up from €43 billion in 2008) and industry (€20 billion in the same year). It is beyond the scope of this book to estimate the extent to which producers themselves benefited from these subsidies (for example, through tolerating greater inefficiency or achieving higher profits), the extent to which the benefits were passed on to consumers or the extent to which they benefited the providers of inputs.

Table 1   Some examples of discriminatory energy subsidies

Fuel	Type of subsidy	Beneficiary	Nature of subsidy	Amount of subsidy
Germany[a]				
Solar power (<100 kW)	Produc-tion	Power producers	Feed-in tariff, depending on where the panel is installed	8.91–12.70 cents per kWh
Biogas	Produc-tion	Biogas producers	Feed-in tariff	13.05–14.88 cents per kWh (depending on the plant size) if from bio-waste 23.14 cents per kWh if from manure 5.66–8.17 cents per kWh (depending on the plant size) if landfill gas 5.66–6.49 cents per kWh (depending on the plant size) if from sewage

[a] http://www.res-legal.eu/search-by-country/germany/single/s/res-e/t/promotion/aid/feed-in-tariff-eeg-feed-in-tariff/lastp/135/

In 2021 the EU Commission released an updated version of the study (EC 2021), concerning energy subsidies in 2019 and 2020. The total amount of energy subsidies in the EU27 totalled €177 billion in 2020, of which €41 billion was for fossil fuels (mainly consumption subsidies) and €71 billion for renewable energy sources (mainly as price support or production subsidies). Unfortunately, this more recent study did not cover the UK. Moreover, as this book is being written, the final report of the 2021 study is available, but the spreadsheet containing all the relevant figures is not yet available on the EU Commission's website. Therefore, in the following analysis we rely on the 2020 study, which uses data up to 2018.

Table 1 (cont.)

Fuel	Type of subsidy	Beneficiary	Nature of subsidy	Amount of subsidy
Italy				
Diesel	Consump-tion	Farmers	Discounted excise tax	13.6 cents per litre versus ordinary rate of 61.7 cents per litre
Diesel	Consump-tion	Farmers	Discounted VAT rate	10 per cent versus ordinary rate of 22 per cent
France[b]				
Nuclear power	Under-funded liabilities	Power producers	Lack of an obligation to set aside sufficient funds to cover for future decommis-sioning costs	€23 billion of earmarked assets compared with €74.1 billion of expected decommis-sioning costs
UK				
All fuels	Consump-tion	Domestic consumers	Discounted VAT rate	All domestic fuel consump-tion is subject to 5 per cent rather than 20 per cent VAT rate

[b] https://www.reuters.com/article/uk-europe-nuclear-idUKKCN0VP2KN?edition-redirect=uk

About a third of the EU27's total subsidies in 2018 are accounted for by Germany (€46 billion), followed by Italy (€26 billion), France (€25 billion) and Spain (€16 billion). The remaining 23 member states were jointly responsible for 29 per cent of EU27's total subsidies. In the UK, energy subsidies in 2018 were about €26 billion.

**Figure 3   Per capita energy subsidies in Europe and
in the G20 in 2018 (euros per capita)**

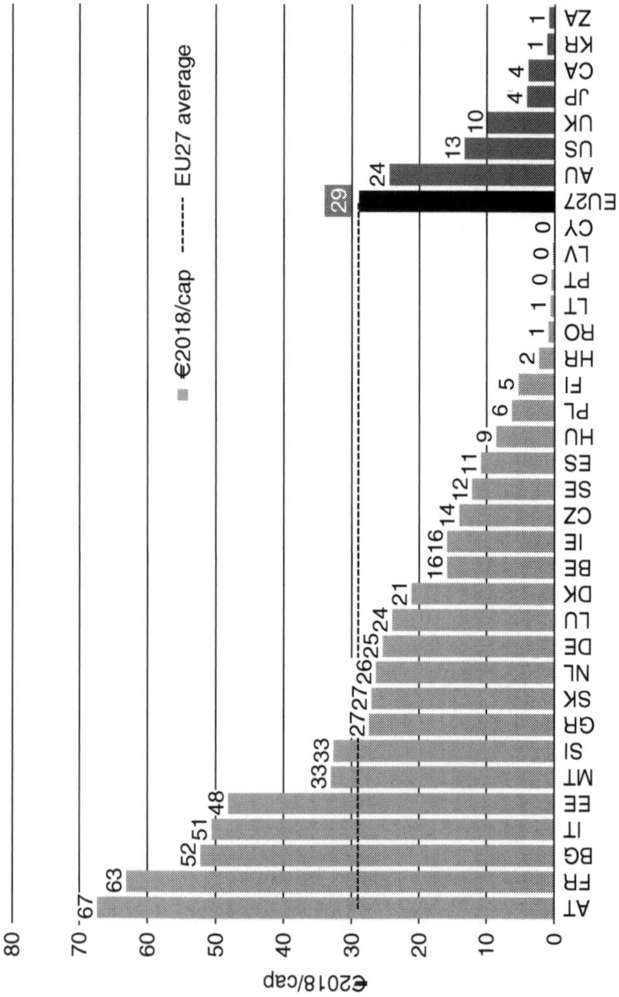

Source: EC (2020a).

Perhaps a better indicator of the level of subsidies is the subsidy per head of population. In 2018, the EU27 average subsidy per head was €355. Germany had the highest rate of subsidy per head (€550), closely followed by Ireland, Finland and Latvia. Energy subsidies in the UK were also around €500 per head. This is summarised in figure 3 together with the figures for the G20.

Subsidies per capita might provide useful information on the extent of rent seeking by the energy industry or other interests or about the social preferences of the electorate. However, in order to determine the potential for subsidies to affect the behaviour of energy producers and consumers, it is necessary to examine their extent per unit of energy.[3] This is complex because subsidies and taxes vary according to the use, the user and the producer of energy. For example, natural gas is either taxed or subsidised depending whether it is for residential or industrial use or for mobility. Also, the amount of tax or subsidy may change according to the kind of industrial processes of which it serves as an input (for example, whether the final product is exposed to international competition, such as steel, or not exposed to international competition, such as electricity). Subsidies to renewable energies vary across different technologies (for example, varying

---

3 To understand the actual impact on production and consumption, it would be necessary to know the elasticity of demand for each fuel type and all the relevant cross-price elasticities of demand. This would include relevant data for all sources, consumers and producers given the variation of subsidies across these dimensions. We do not attempt that kind of modelling here.

for wind, solar and bio-energies) and even the size of the generating plants (rooftop solar panels are often subsidised more generously than solar fields).

With all these caveats, based on the figures from the EU-sponsored study on energy prices and costs in the EU and G20 member states, subsidies by primary energy sources in the EU27 and the UK have been estimated. As in the case of taxes, subsidies have been estimated per unit of energy. Figure 4 shows the results for the EU27 and the UK.

Figure 4   Subsidies by energy sources in the UK and the EU27 (2018)

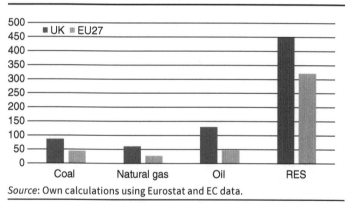

Source: Own calculations using Eurostat and EC data.

In general, subsidies are higher in the UK than in the EU27, although there is significant heterogeneity across the EU's member states. Subsidies in the UK and the EU27 respectively average €86 and €44 per TOE for coal; €61 and €27 per TOE of natural gas; €130 and €47 per TOE of oil; and €448 and €320 per TOE of renewable energy sources. The UK and EU member states follow a wide array of different policies when it comes to subsidising energy sources. For example, fossil fuels receive very small subsidies in some member states, but a TOE of coal is subsidised by €263 in Sweden, a TOE of natural gas by €64 in Germany and a TOE of oil by as much as €314 in Estonia. Subsidies to renewables are consistently higher than those to fossil fuels. Although Finland and Sweden provide subsidies of little more than €20 per TOE to renewables, Germany provides subsidies of €674 per TOE to renewables. Subsidies to renewables in Malta are more than €1,000 per TOE.

As discussed above, energy subsidies do not relate to any assessment of environmental externalities. Both fossil fuels and renewable sources receive subsidies. Furthermore, there is a very wide variation of subsidies within the renewable category, as can be seen in figure 5.

Figure 5   Subsidies by renewable energy technologies in the UK and the EU27

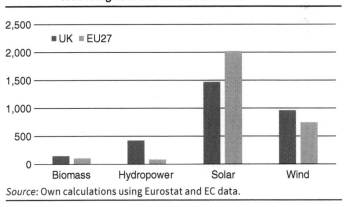

Source: Own calculations using Eurostat and EC data.

Solar power receives the highest subsidies. They amount to €1,468 per TOE in the UK and €2,019 per TOE in the EU27. Wind follows closely with €961 per TOE in the UK and €743 per TOE in the EU27. Hydropower and bio-energies on the other hand receive more moderate subsidies.[4]

Figure 6 shows the breakdown of the average household's power bill by component. In Great Britain, for example, green subsidies accounted for about 21 per cent of the total price. A combination of renewable subsidies, taxes and network charges account for more than half the price in most EU member states and the UK.

Figure 6   Breakdown of incumbents' standard electricity offers for households in capital cities – November/December 2019 (per cent)

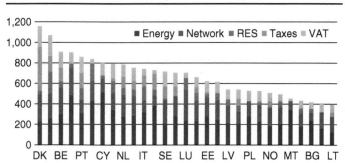

Source: ACER (2020). Note: we have used data from 2019, rather than 2020 (available in ACER 2021), because this latter was an exceptional year due to the effects of Covid-19 as well as the exceptional measures that were taken by many countries to reduce the cost of electricity.

---

4   It should be noted that subsidies awarded on new projects tend to be significantly lower than historical subsidies as current support schemes are lower. This is partly because of the reduced costs of the relevant technologies. Over time, therefore, subsidies to renewables will reduce naturally.

Net energy subsidies

Taxes and subsidies change the relative prices of goods and services and so affect both their supply and demand. However, taxes and subsidies on the same fuel source for a given use can offset each other. If a product is both taxed and subsidised, what ultimately matters is the net tax or subsidy.

Having estimated the average taxes and subsidies that are levied upon energy sources, the net amount of taxes or subsidies can be calculated. If subsidies exceed taxes, a particular energy source can be thought of as being in receipt of a net subsidy. This would only be appropriate from an economic welfare-maximising perspective if there were positive externalities associated with the energy sources, which, as explained above, is highly unlikely. If taxes are greater than subsidies, the fuel source is subject to a net tax. This would be appropriate if there are negative externalities arising from the use of the fuel.

There is an additional complexity in estimating the net subsidies. While taxes are generally levied upon the final price of energy, subsidies may be designed to benefit either the production or the consumption of energy. Therefore, taxes and subsidies may fall upon (and have an incidence upon) different subjects. Moreover, some subsidies (particularly those concerning the production of electricity) are financed by, in effect, mandatory payments from energy consumers to energy producers. Their actual impact, from an economic point of view, is indistinguishable from a tax on electricity consumers in general coupled with a subsidy to renewable energy producers. An algebraic sum of taxes and subsidies therefore provides only a proxy for whether a specific source of an energy has been, on average, taxed or, on average, subsidised. Net energy subsidies by energy source for the UK and the EU27 are shown in figure 7.

Figure 7   Net subsidies by energy source in the UK and the EU27 (2018)

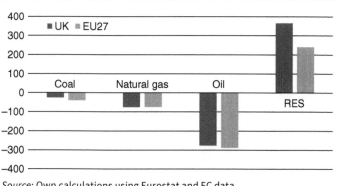

Source: Own calculations using Eurostat and EC data.

As figure 7 shows, although fossil fuels are subsidised, the impact of taxes outweighs that of subsidies on average. In other words, energy consumers pay a price which is greater than that which they would pay in the absence of taxes or subsidies. The opposite is true for renewable energies which are in receipt of considerable net subsidies.

The UK tends to both subsidise more and tax energy sources more than the EU27 does. But when the effect of taxes and subsidies is combined, the outcome is close to that in the EU. This is shown in figure 8. In the EU, net taxes on coal are more than in the UK (€40 per TOE versus €25 per TOE in the EU). Net subsidies are almost identical for natural gas and oil. Renewable energy sources are large recipients of net subsidies: each TOE of green energy is subsidised by €364 in the UK and €240 in the EU.

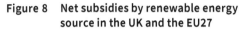

Figure 8   Net subsidies by renewable energy source in the UK and the EU27

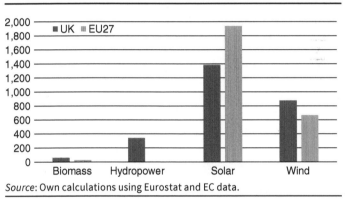

Source: Own calculations using Eurostat and EC data.

This analysis raises several questions. Fossil fuels are in receipt of large-scale subsidies as well as taxes being charged on their use. The net effect on different fossil fuels is different. Furthermore, subsidies vary considerably according to the use to which fossil fuels are put. Natural gas and other sources of energy for domestic consumption, for example, receive subsidies not given to the same fuels used for other purposes. It is possible, for example, that hydrocarbons used for domestic heating are subsidised overall while hydrocarbons used in cars are taxed heavily overall. The net taxes on diesel for farm use are far lower than those on diesel for other uses. This leads to extremely inefficient use of fossil fuels that may be over-consumed in some uses and under-consumed in other uses. It also makes interpretation of the aggregate data difficult.

The optimal amount of taxes on fossil fuels depends on the external costs that their combustion inflicts on society. At this stage of the analysis, it would appear that, on average, fossil fuels, particularly oil, pay more taxes than they receive in subsidies both in the UK and the EU27. However, the level of taxes does not necessarily reflect the externalities incurred by their use.

When it comes to renewables, subsidies vary hugely depending on the form of renewable energy. We would argue that there is no place for renewable subsidies in a carbon-reduction agenda. If there are subsidies for renewables and if these are differentiated between types of renewable energy, the only grounds for differentiation would be if the amount of carbon emissions underlying the conventional energy generation or consumption that is displaced by renewables themselves differs.

The current situation is likely to give rise to perverse results. For example, even when it is cheaper to reduce carbon emissions by energy efficiency measures rather than by substituting hydrocarbons with renewables, the latter option may be chosen because of the net subsidies to renewables. Other carbon-free technologies – such as nuclear power or carbon capture, sequestration and utilisation – may be displaced because they are unsubsidised, or less subsidised, than renewables. Car drivers are incentivised to reduce carbon emissions, whereas those using farm vehicles or, in some cases, truck drivers and airlines are not.

Excessive taxation may even lead to inefficient cuts in either energy use or emissions. The social as well as private costs from fossil fuels should be compared with the benefits, both private and social, arising from their use. This is why environmental negotiations, even under the most aggressive targets, do not ask the parties to immediately cut emissions down to zero – they set a gradual phaseout of emissions. Under the Paris Agreement, the target of keeping the temperature increase 'well below' 2 °C, and possibly to 1.5 °C, translates into 'net zero' targets by the middle of this century. Both the UK and the EU27 have committed to cut their own emissions by 55 per cent by 2030 – not by 100 per cent in 2022 – implicitly recognizing that environmental goals should be pursued while not giving up other socially valuable goals, including economic growth, poverty reduction and the development of a prosperous, inclusive society. Hence, the optimal amount of carbon emissions is not necessarily zero. Even the most aggressive goals are not framed as 'zero emissions' – they are framed as '*net* zero emissions', meaning that there may be scope for keeping in place carbon-emitting technologies as long as their emissions are either captured, or offset by carbon sinks or other forms of atmospheric carbon capture (Gambhir and Tavoni 2019).

Overall, the net taxes on coal and gas are small – perhaps smaller than the externality arising from carbon emissions. That would mean those taxes are inadequate for achieving the objective of ensuring that emitters pay social and private costs of fuel use. We consider this in the next chapter.

If it is the case that climate change is an urgent and important problem, it would be fair to say that the policies being used to address the problem are chaotic. Neither the pattern of net subsidies, nor the mix of taxes and subsidies that gives rise to it, arises from a master-stroke of central planning which, somehow, ensures that the right relative prices are charged for different fuels. Instead, it would appear that the pattern of interventions is determined by flawed political decision-making processes which respond to political pressures and special interests and the public preference for visible subsidies funded by invisible general taxation rather than highly visible taxes on carbon emissions (Umit and Schaffer 2020).

In the next chapter, we will investigate whether fossil fuels are taxed enough or too much to compensate the externalities arising from carbon emissions on average and examine the subsidies to renewables further. To do this, we need to make assumptions about the externalities from carbon emissions.

5 FROM GOVERNMENT FAILURE TO A MORE RATIONAL CLIMATE CHANGE POLICY

Fuel subsidies and government failure

There have been attempts at the international level to eliminate subsidies to fossil fuels. The Paris Agreement on climate change, signed in 2015, included commitments to report on fossil fuel subsidies and to track progress in phasing them out. While vague, these commitments seem to include any form of direct as well as indirect support to fossil fuels, such as production subsidies, consumption subsidies, reduced VAT and other forms of tax relief. Countries also agreed to provide clear and understandable information to the public regarding the scope and scale of fossil fuel subsidies and efforts to address them. G20 leaders at the Pittsburgh Summit in 2009 pledged to:

> phase out and rationalize over the medium term ineffi-
> cient fossil fuel subsidies while providing targeted support
> for the poorest. Inefficient fossil fuel subsidies encourage
> wasteful consumption, reduce our energy security, im-
> pede investment in clean energy sources and undermine
> efforts to deal with the threat of climate change.[1]

---

1   https://ec.europa.eu/archives/commission_2010-2014/president/pdf/
    statement_20090826_en_2.pdf

However, in the last ten years, there has been little (if any) change in fossil fuel subsidies in the EU or in the UK. A new pledge was signed at the recent COP26 conference in Glasgow. The final declaration calls the parties to accelerate 'efforts towards ... the phase-out of *inefficient* fossil fuel subsidies'[2] (emphasis added). There is no reason to assume it will be any more successful than previous attempts. In fact, as part of the relief packages during the Covid-19 crisis and, later, during the European energy crunch in late 2021, several governments increased energy subsidies that supported the consumption of fossil fuels.

Rentschler and Bazilian (2016) point to the impact of removing fuel subsidies on the poor as a particular obstacle to reform. In addition, well-organised and better-off interest groups, among both consumers and producers, make reform difficult. The influence of the latter is exactly as public choice economics would predict (see, for example, Yandle 2010). It is not so clear, though, why reform packages that involve compensating the poor – for example, by reducing other taxes on the poor – cannot be combined with the removal of fuel subsidies in a way that would lead to electoral support, greater economic efficiency and better environmental outcomes. It is possible that there is a status quo bias and that fuel subsidies are more transparent to their recipients than equivalent general reductions in taxation that might be financed by a removal of subsidies. The *gilet jaune* protests in France demonstrated that fuel

---

2   https://unfccc.int/sites/default/files/resource/cop26_auv_2f_cover_dec ision.pdf

taxes and subsidies are highly transparent and changes lead to strong reactions. Equivalent tax cuts, financed by reductions in energy subsidies, may be less obvious in the eyes of their recipients. Ultimately, the promise of future tax cuts may not be reliable enough to make acceptable a corresponding certain and immediate increase in fuel taxes or reduction in subsidies. Furthermore, subsidies may be unevenly distributed with those households who receive particularly large subsidies being especially sensitive to their loss.

These pressures may explain why fossil fuel subsidies have not been phased out. But why have governments used new forms of subsidy for the development of renewables rather than the more economically rational approach of introducing carbon taxes on carbon-intensive fuels? This is an especially pertinent question given the desire of governments with large deficits and debts to raise revenue from new sources. Again, the answer may lie in public choice economics and lobbying, especially from businesses. Research, for example, by Kang (2016), Li et al. (2019) and Lockwood et al. (2020) in relation to countries as diverse as the US, Japan and the UK respectively suggests that industry lobby groups are important in promoting support for subsidies for renewables.

The attitude of the Green Party in the UK in relation to fuel subsidies is interesting. The Green Party manifesto in 2019 was a very comprehensive document with sophisticated economic arguments being used in some places. However, it did not suggest removing the implicit subsidy on domestic fuel consumption in the UK. It did, however, propose a progressively increasing general carbon tax and the removal of the VAT exemption from aviation. This is not surprising from a public choice perspective. The charging of VAT on domestic fuel use, which is a transparent tax on consumers, is rejected in favour of a tax which is likely to be largely hidden from consumers. This would be predicted by the literature on tax transparency within public choice economics. The experience of the Conservative government in trying to remove fuel subsidies, described earlier, also illustrates the problems.

Even more informative is the reaction of the UK and most EU member states to the energy crunch in late 2021. Confronted by rapidly increasing natural gas and electricity prices, most governments reacted by subsidising households and businesses in order to offset the price increases. Where that has not happened, major political parties have proposed it. As inconsistent as it may seem, heads of governments gathered in Glasgow for COP26 and committed to phasing out fossil fuel subsidies and the use of fossil fuels. They then returned home and made proposals to use taxpayer funds to make energy artificially cheaper. Table 2 summarises the various forms of interventions that some European countries and the UK have introduced in the second half of 2021, including both monetary transfers and provisional regulations. For example, the UK introduced a £500 million fund to help the vulnerable customers on top of the existing schemes, such as the Warm Home Discount. It also bailed out several energy retailers that went bust because of high prices and the existing price caps (Sgaravatti et al. 2021).

Table 2   National policies to shield consumers from rising energy prices

Country	1	2	3	4	5	6	7
Belgium	✓	✓		✓			✓
Cyprus	✓				✓		
Czech Republic	✓			✓			
Estonia	✓			✓			
France			✓	✓		✓	✓
Germany	✓			✓	✓		
Greece				✓	✓		
Hungary							
Ireland	✓			✓			✓
Italy	✓			✓	✓		
Latvia				✓			
Lithuania		✓		✓			✓
Luxembourg							
Netherlands	✓						
Norway				✓			
Poland	✓	✓		✓			
Portugal	✓		✓		✓		
Romania		✓	✓	✓		✓	
Spain	✓	✓	✓	✓		✓	
UK			✓				✓

Policies: 1, Reduced energy tax/VAT; 2, Retail price regulation; 3, Wholesale price regulation; 4, Transfers to vulnerable groups; 5, Mandate to state-owned firms; 6, Windfall profits tax/regulation; 7, Other.

Source: Sgaravatti et al. (2021).

These policies became even more ubiquitous (and costly) after 24 February 2022. Governments temporarily reduced energy taxation, subsidised energy consumption and energy efficiency (without even realising that this is inherently contradictory), or subdised investments in energy technologies aimed at reducing the reliance on natural gas. Energy policy became even more driven by short- and long-run policy objectives that have little (or nothing) to do with the aims of making energy more reliable, sustainable and cheaper. When the situation will become normalised, most of these measures will be phased out, while the legacy of others will remain for years or decades. The need to reconcile taxes and subsidies with the stated goals of energy policy (competitiveness, security and sustainability) will emerge as a main issue in the public policy debate.

There is no doubt that current policy in relation to fossil fuel subsidies is a significant government failure. Given the government's declared objective of reducing carbon emissions, there is no economic efficiency argument for subsidising fossil fuels even if fossil fuels are also taxed. For any given desired level of net taxes, a better policy would be to remove subsidies and reduce taxes, combined with redistributive measures, if appropriate. Furthermore, an efficient carbon-reduction policy would not differentiate taxes and subsidies on energy sources depending upon who the consumer is.

Carbon taxes and global warming

Following the elimination of energy subsidies of all forms, there then remains the question of how we try to ensure that energy users pay the full costs of energy use, including those arising from externalities such as global warming. Given the nature of carbon emissions and associated global warming, carbon taxes or cap-and-trade schemes should certainly be considered as the 'least-worst' device to address the problem. Other approaches to reducing carbon emissions have been proposed but have limits. They may, however, be effective in dealing with other forms of emissions from traditional fuels.

Polycentric approaches and their limits

Carbon emissions are different from many forms of pollution: they are global in their extent. There is no obvious solution to the problems caused by carbon emissions that could derive from better legal definition and enforcement of property rights.

Nevertheless, there are approaches that harness the principles of institutional economics and what was described by Elinor Ostrom as 'polycentric' governance.[3] There are two important features of such an approach. The first is that there are several layers of governance, each with responsibility that is appropriate to its level. For example, at the global level, governance might involve an institution through which global agreement about general principles was reached with information being provided by the global institution about compliance and scientific matters. At lower levels of governance, specific approaches

---

3   See Ostrom (2012) for a specific short discussion of climate change, especially pages 82 and 86.

to reducing carbon emissions might be designed and implemented. A second feature of Ostrom's thinking was that some of the impacts of climate change were concentrated in local areas, and local communities and politicians at this level might therefore be a focus for action. This might be through carbon-reduction measures, but also through various forms of adaptation – or simply the restoration of pre-existing woodlands which can help deal more effectively with the effects of more extreme weather events. Change at the business, individual and cultural level may also help people change lifestyles in ways that will reduce carbon emissions.

The authors would argue that polycentric approaches are important because of the known imperfections of political processes, even in the best-governed countries. However, given the enormous potential costs of climate change, its nature as a widespread externality and the likely difficulty of coordinating local solutions on a large enough scale, there are limits to polycentric approaches and a carbon tax is therefore justified as the particular response to carbon emissions in the UK and the EU. In particular, a carbon tax (or equivalent forms of carbon pricing, such as a cap-and-trade scheme or a hybrid system) is definitely superior to picking-winner policies which are common in the UK, in Europe and elsewhere.

Towards a more efficient tax regime

The use of a carbon tax as the main, or perhaps only, device used to reduce carbon emissions has the advantage of encouraging consumers and producers to reduce carbon emissions in the most efficient way. It also encourages those who can make reductions in emissions most cheaply and/or value their ability to emit carbon the least to make the most substantial reductions. The approach does not presuppose that the government knows which technologies should be adopted and who should reduce carbon emissions by how much. A Centre for Policy Studies report notes that Pigovian taxes do work. It credits the Landfill Tax and the Carbon Price Support as being responsible for what is describes as a 'staggering' reduction in domestic emissions in energy supply and waste management (Ives 2021: 27).

These considerations also hold for other instruments aimed at pricing externalities such as cap-and-trade schemes, although there may be reasons to prefer taxing over carbon trading or vice versa as is discussed by Weitzman (1974) and Goulder and Schein (2013). From here on, we will use the expression 'carbon taxation' while accepting that our conclusions could equally lead some to conclude that the objective of reducing carbon emissions efficiently could be better served using alternative but similar approaches that do not discriminate between technologies.

While carbon taxes might be the most efficient ways to reduce emissions, there are still serious drawbacks in their use to try to achieve an alignment of social costs and benefits (Metcalf 2021). Carbon taxes might be described as 'the best of a bad bunch' – but they are the best by a considerable distance.

The social costs of carbon emissions are very difficult to estimate and hugely uncertain. The costs will be different in different parts of the world. There is no effective way of even discovering, let alone aggregating, the preferences for and aversion to global warming across different persons in different geographical regions. The impacts of carbon emissions today are also very long term and their future costs are even more uncertain than their present costs. In addition, we do not know how the ability of people to adapt to climate change and the cost of reducing emissions will evolve over time. These are not challenges that can be overcome: the information necessary to solve these problems is not there waiting to be found – it does not exist.

Nevertheless, it can be said that some types of policy are more likely than others to achieve their goals, and at a lower cost. In addition, a better policy should leave some room for trial and error, not just as regards the best technological mix to reduce emissions (which will change over time, as technological progress provides us with new solutions) but also with regard to the best mix between mitigation (i.e. reducing emissions in order to keep global temperatures from increasing) and adaptation (i.e. developing better ways to live in a warmer world). We are making a judgement that, despite its shortcomings, a carbon tax is a better approach than not using the price mechanism to reduce carbon emissions at all. A carbon tax regime should be regarded as a 'more efficient' regime than alternatives rather than as an 'optimal' regime.

The objective should be to set the carbon tax so that it reflects the externalities arising from carbon emissions. The alternative is, in effective, to assume that the right price for carbon emissions is zero. The calculations below estimate the impact on the price of different fuels from aligning taxes with the social costs of the fuel.

In the following discussion, for the sake of comparison, we rely on the most recent estimates of the value of external costs from the use of energy sources. Estimates are based on values from EC (2020a–c) for coal, natural gas and renewable energies and on values from EC (2019) for oil. A few methodological explanations are required.

EC (2019) provides an estimate of the total value of externalities from the transport sector with particular reference to road transport. Such externalities include environment or health-related costs (such as climate change, local pollution, the loss of habitat, etc.) and other costs that depend upon the actual traffic conditions (accidents, congestion, infrastructure use, etc.). Only the former is included in the following analysis, as the latter are independent of the fuel used. Indeed, these costs should be captured by forms of road-user charging. The whole external cost from road transport (net of accidents, congestion, infrastructure, and the like) is assumed to be attributable to oil. Hence, external costs from oil consumption are estimated as the ratio between total external costs from road transport and total oil consumption in the UK and the EU27. Even though oil is also employed in uses other than transportation, this seems a reasonable approach, at least as a first approximation.

The European Commission (EC) also provides detailed estimates of the external costs from electricity and heat-generation technologies in its report on energy prices and costs (EC 2020a–c). Because of the way these estimates are produced by the EC, a number of simplifying assumptions are made in our calculations.[4] The principle is that we have focused on those externalities that are measurable. Externalities by energy sources are estimated for the EU27 as well as for the G20, but no country-level data is provided by the EC study. The UK's costs are assumed to be equal to those of the EU27. This assumption could be questioned: the technological level of energy-producing and energy-consuming processes varies across EU member states and the UK. However, internal variations are small relative to the uncertainties in the estimate.

Figure 9   Net subsidies after internalisation by energy source in the UK and the EU27

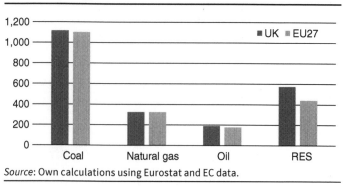

Source: Own calculations using Eurostat and EC data.

---

4   Please contact the authors for more information.

It should also be noted that the external costs estimated by the EC are not simply those relating to carbon emissions. We consider this further below.

An important consequence of the above discussion is that, while indications of the appropriate level of taxation of carbon-intensive fuels can be drawn, we cannot derive precise estimates. The textbook Pigovian tax designed to align social and private costs cannot, in reality, be determined precisely. We will, nevertheless, demonstrate how we can move closer to a welfare-maximising position than the current arbitrary mix of taxes and subsidies.

Figure 9 shows the extent of net subsidies for all energy sources after allowing for externalities. Figure 10 shows the net subsidy for different renewable energy sources.

Figure 10 Net subsidies after internalisation by renewable energy source in the UK and the EU27

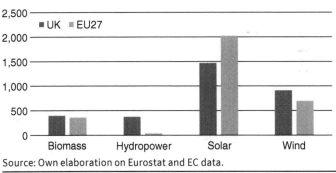

Source: Own elaboration on Eurostat and EC data.

An intuitive way to interpret these graphs is to think of the columns as deviations from optimal pricing: a positive deviation means that an energy source is over-subsidised (i.e.

its price does not reflect the private as well as social costs, either because it is the recipient of undue subsidies or because the price does not fully internalise externalities). A negative deviation suggests that prices, after taxes and subsidies, are above the optimal level, or that the source is over-taxed.

Figures 9 and 10 show that all energy sources are subsidised, according to our definition. This includes renewables. However, the degree of subsidy varies considerably across energy sources. It is likely that the oil subsidy is relatively small because of the high levels of taxation on motoring and that the subsidy on coal is high because of the high levels of social costs. The degree of subsidy after allowing for social costs is similar in the EU27 and the UK.

Oil prices are the closest to their optimal level: in fact, both in the UK and in the EU27 a TOE of oil costs about €200 less than it would if all social costs were reflected in its price. That would translate into an additional tax of approximately €0.18 per litre of diesel and €0.15 per litre of gasoline.

It is important to note that a move towards a more efficient regime of taxes and subsidies would not have the same impact on all consumers. Domestic heating oil, for example, costs around €0.5 per litre. The addition of both VAT and an additional tax of the magnitude suggested above would increase the price of heating oil to around €0.70–0.75 per litre. This is hugely below the cost of petroleum for transport, which suffers from much higher levels of taxes already.[5]

---

5   Though it should be noted that part of these taxes could be regarded as an appropriate contribution to the cost of the road network and taxes might also be levied on petrol for other reasons – for example, because the demand for fuel is price inelastic.

It is highly likely that, if a carbon tax were charged on oil products that reflected social costs, there would be a significant rise in the price of oil for some purposes (such as domestic heating). If domestic heating oil with the addition of VAT is representative of the average price of oil per litre, it is quite possible that the price of some types of fuel, including fuel for cars, would have their taxes reduced. Indeed, it was observed after the publication of the Stern Report on climate change in the UK that its proposals would actually lead to a reduction in the rate of fuel duty (see Wellings 2012). Our conclusions are consistent with this earlier work.

On the other hand, farmers who can buy red diesel, which is subject to a different tax regime, would see a considerable increase in the price they paid as would businesses using oil to provide energy for industrial production or electricity generation.[6] Similarly, as noted above, kerosene used by airlines rarely attracts even the normal consumption taxes which are designed to be levied on all goods and services and the cost of kerosene would therefore rise significantly.

Natural gas is also below the price that would prevail if it reflected all social costs. In fact, in the case of natural gas, the taxes and subsidies and the external costs are each lower than for oil, but the net effect is similar. Overall, there is a net subsidy after allowing for social costs of about €300 per TOE or €0.27 per cubic metre. This would

---

6   In this case, this increase in cost would be offset by reductions in the costs of renewable obligations and other highly opaque mechanisms for taxing electricity produced using fossil fuels.

lead, for example, to an increase in domestic gas prices of around 55 per cent in the UK. About one-third of this increase would be represented by the imposition of VAT at the full rate. Of course, energy bills would fall to partly counteract this rise because of the removal of renewable obligations. These calculations were made before recent events in energy markets. The required uplift in prices would be much less at the time of publication – certainly as a percentage of the price.

Coal is especially heavily susidised. Coal subsidies almost fully offset the impact of environmental taxation. However, the externalities from coal (especially in relation to climate change and local pollution) are large. As a result, a TOE of coal costs more than €1,000 less than it should. This is equivalent to €528 per tonne of coal. The removal of subsidies, together with the imposition of a tax that reflected the social costs of coal use would lead to the price of coal rising from about €80 a tonne to €600 a tonne.

Renewable sources of energy receive considerable net subsidies. As discussed above, renewable energy does not provide any positive externalities. Under certain conditions, they may reduce the negative externalities arising from fossil fuels. They can create negative externalities, too, for example by making electricity generation less predictable or by increasing network and backup costs in order to manage intermittent production (Stagnaro 2015). Rather than subsidising renewables, the government should tax fossil fuels appropriately.

Allowing for all social costs, each TOE of renewables is over-subsidised by over €440 in the EU27 and almost €600 in the UK. However, there are considerable differences between different renewable energy sources. Biomass and hydro power are the least subsidised (hydro power in the EU27 is hardly subsidised at all when taxes and externalities are factored in). On the other hand, wind and solar power have large subsidies. Wind power has a subsidy of €700 per TOE in the EU and €900 per TOE in the UK. Solar power has a subsidy of €1,500 per TOE in the UK and €2,000 per TOE in the EU: this corresponds to €128.9 and €172.0 per MWh, respectively. This should be compared with the average cost of a MWh paid by households of €128.3 per MWh in the EU27 and €151.2 per MWh in the UK in 2019 (net of taxes and levies).

The recent increase in energy prices seems to obscure the role of taxes and subsidies in raising prices and distorting market signals. Taxes have been temporarily reduced and subsidies (both to the production, consumption and conservation of energy) have been increased. But sooner or later this messy situation will have to be rationalised and the effects of an incoherent policy will become evident.

Practical applications of carbon pricing

In theory, if the estimates of social costs are correct, carbon taxes could be charged and subsidies removed to the extent proposed above. There are, however, arguments against such an approach.

Firstly, the extent of the social costs can, of course, be disputed. In fact, the EU's own estimate is higher than that in much of the literature. Commonly accepted values for the social cost of carbon fall in the range US$50–100 per tonne of CO_2 but several studies find lower values of around US$30 per tonne of CO_2 (Nordhaus 2017) and estimates have not increased over time (Tol 2021a). This should be compared with the average price of a tonne of CO_2 in the EU's cap-and-trade scheme (of which the UK was also a member until 31 December 2020). In 2019, emitting a tonne of CO_2 cost around €20. This rose to almost €30 in late 2020 (despite the Covid-induced recession). At the time of writing, allowances are at or above €80 per tonne of CO_2.

The estimate of external costs by the EC, both in the transport study (EC 2019) and in the electricity and heating study (EC 2020a–c), is €100 per tonne of CO_2. A lower estimate would lead to lower increases in the cost of carbon-intensive energy. The precise level of externalities from carbon emissions is impossible to estimate for the reasons discussed above. However, what is clear is that the current pattern of taxes and subsidies is arbitrary and totally unrelated to any rational assessment of social costs. This is harmful because it means that any attempt to reduce carbon emissions comes at a greater economic cost (or, equivalently, for a given economic cost, there will be less of a reduction in carbon emissions). Insofar as policy is designed to ensure that the poor can afford energy, this is more effectively achieved by cash transfers than by subsidising energy use.

Secondly, the whole framework of Pigovian taxes can be disputed given our inability to estimate social costs in the absence of market information about actual individual and social preferences regarding the state of the world a few decades from now. Much of the economic literature has performed cost–benefit analyses of future climate change and climate-mitigating policies by relying on extreme scenarios, thereby contributing little to more informed policymaking (Tol 2021b; Pielke and Ritchie 2020). There are then, of course, political difficulties in implementing a carbon tax.

Thirdly, the EU estimates of social costs include costs not associated with carbon emissions and global warming. These may include, for example, particulate emissions. There are other approaches that can be used to deal with more localised externalities. If the carbon tax only reflected the social costs of carbon emissions, through its impact on global warming, it would be lower than the estimates above.

Fourthly, a case can be made for not fully reflecting all social costs in taxes for trade-exposed industries in order to prevent carbon leakage through the substitution of carbon intensive production by imports that are equally or more carbon intensive (Böhringer et al. 2017; Fischer and Fox 2012; Stagnaro 2020). An alternative approach would be to use a carbon border adjustment by which carbon-intensive imports were taxed if they came from countries that had no form of carbon pricing.

Despite these problems, it is helpful to examine the extent of the change in absolute and relative prices that would be necessary, if this approach to reducing carbon emissions were taken, as we have done above and explore further below.

The latest estimates from the International Monetary Fund (Parry et al. 2021) suggest that petrol and diesel are over-taxed in most EU member states and in the UK. This is especially so if the costs of congestion are excluded as they do not depend on the fuel source and should be charged for separately (an electric vehicle produces the same effects on congestion as any other vehicle). As regards the UK, Adam et al. (2021) found an implicit carbon price for road fuels and electricity well above the commonly used values of €50–100 per tonne of CO_2. For example, British households pay an implicit price of almost £150 per tonne of CO_2 on their electricity consumption. Natural gas prices, on the other hand, do not fully internalise their environmental costs. British drivers also pay an implicit cost of above £200 per tonne of CO_2 on gasoline and diesel. This suggests that a carbon tax would lead to lower costs for road users, potentially lower electricity bills (though this is complex), but definitely higher natural gas costs.

A transparent carbon tax would affect relative prices dramatically as well as affecting the total cost of energy use. If we do use the EU's own estimate of the external costs from energy use, there is no doubt that there would be an increase in the cost of energy overall. The increase would be unequal across energy sources: it would be more modest for oil, natural gas, hydro power and biomass as compared with for coal, wind power and solar power. All else being equal, this would result in a reduction of energy demand in general and a change in demand patterns away from coal, solar and wind and towards natural gas, hydro power and biomass.

In any policy approach, nuclear power would be considered in the same way as other renewables. We do not believe it should be subsidised because there is no positive externality. A higher price for carbon-intensive fuels might make nuclear viable, but it should not be especially favoured – or penalised – by government.

Overall, if users of fossil fuels were taxed in such a way that prices reflected social costs, there would be a significant increase in costs to consumers and businesses. Costs to businesses would ultimately be passed on in higher consumer prices. Nevertheless, pricing carbon in this way is likely to be the cheapest and most efficient way to reduce carbon emissions. Alternative ways of reducing emissions that governments are pursuing will almost certainly be more expensive if they succeed in their objectives. The costs of these alternative approaches are, however, opaque. Taxing carbon emissions allows individuals and businesses to reduce emissions in the manner cheapest for them. The dramatic change in relative prices that would arise from a carbon tax and the elimination of other interventions would be a benefit of a change of approach. Subsidising renewables and nuclear power or banning or promoting particular technologies leads individuals and businesses to reduce carbon emissions in ways that will be less efficient and may sometimes be counter-productive.

Political decision makers can therefore read this book and decide whether they wish to propose a transparent approach to carbon reduction to the electorate. Electors can then make a judgement about whether the benefits are worth the costs. The fact that politicians propose less transparent approaches that will cost much more reflects poorly on the political system, but is predicted by public choice economics (Kollmann and Schneider 2010; Umit and Schaffer 2020). This book makes no judgement on whether the government should use a carbon tax, a cap-and-trade scheme, or any other instrument to price carbon. However, we do argue that, if the government is to attempt to reduce carbon emissions, pricing carbon is the approach it should take. Other approaches will be less efficient and mislead the electorate. All existing carbon-reduction measures, except cap-and-trade schemes, should be replaced with a carbon tax or by an extension of the cap-and-trade mechanisms if the policy objective is to reduce carbon emissions.

A tax on carbon emissions will, however, raise revenue that can be used to lower other taxes. We would propose that such tax reductions are directly linked to carbon tax revenues in any legislation. There are two costs for consumers from imposing carbon taxes. The first arises from individuals and businesses making decisions that involve moving to sources of fuel that, net of taxes, are costlier. If a household moves from a diesel car to a battery-powered car charged using wind-generated electricity, for example, this will have an upfront cost to the household which cannot be recovered and would be balanced against the gains from reduced carbon emissions. The second cost is that of the tax itself for those households and businesses that use fuels that lead to emissions. This second cost is not an economic resource cost, as such: it is a transfer. The revenue arising from the carbon taxes should be used to reduce taxes that have roughly the same redistributive effect as the carbon tax – for example, excise duties, national insurance contributions or the general rate of VAT. The revenue generated by the tax should not be seen as the cost to households of imposing the tax. Indeed, the bigger economic resource cost arises from people changing their fuel use and *not* paying the tax. This is, of course, a counter-intuitive argument.

An alternative framework for dealing with local externalities

Estimating the value of externalities from different forms of energy production and consumption is complex and uncertain. As a result, as noted above, the use of carbon taxes to deal with the externalities of global warming has serious defects. However, it appears to the authors that other approaches are more defective. Pigovian taxes should only be used where no other approach is possible. We note in this section that it might be possible to deal with those externalities that are more local in scope than global warming through other means and so the taxes discussed above could be reduced appropriately so that they only reflect carbon emissions and not other externalities.

The emitting of particulates is one such source of local externalities. While externalities from particulates may be very difficult to estimate, at least some attempt can be used to model preferences using market values given that damage can be relatively localised and immediate: this is not true of the social costs of carbon emissions.

If the social costs from particulates are relatively localised, it may be more efficient to deal with them ways other than the imposition of Pigovian taxes. Competition between local government areas with different tax and charging regimes will also allow residents to express their preferences for different levels of pollution. Residents who prefer higher levels of pollution and lower taxes can express their preferences both by voting for a local government regime that will bring that situation about or by moving from one area to another (Wooders 1999; Mieszkowski and Zodrow 1989; Somin 2020).

Other externalities from power generation and consumption can also be addressed using markets or market-based mechanisms. For example, when power producers harm local residents by reducing the value of real estate or by impacting the landscape, local residents may be compensated by the producers. Several traffic-related externalities do not depend on the fuel usage per se, but on congestion: road pricing would be a better alternative to fuel taxation to deal with this.

Thus, many externalities arising from fuel consumption and production that are not related to carbon emissions do not need general national government policies at all. The problems are not significantly different from a range of other scenarios where economic activity by one party has an impact on another party such as potash mining or coal mining. Even if Pigovian taxes are used, if they are levied at the local level, it is more likely that local preferences will be satisfied. Externalities with a local impact do not justify either taxes or subsidies at the national level. They require a legal, institutional and constitutional framework which allows the maximum scope for preferences to be expressed through various bargaining and charging mechanisms at local level.

Annex: The implicit cost of carbon from taxes and subsidies

The above discussion relies on subjective estimates of the external costs from the combustion of fossil fuels. Another way of looking at the issue is by estimating the implicit cost of carbon, i.e. the effective price that is attached to the carbon dioxide emissions from (taxed) fossil fuels or to the avoided emissions from the use of (subsidised) renewable energies. That also relies on some simplifying assumptions. The most important ones are the following:

- We will assume that climate change is the single most important externality from the use of fossil fuels. Therefore, we will assume that (net) taxation of fossil fuels, i.e. the difference between taxes and subsidies, is only intended to price carbon emissions. Other externalities do exist, such as particulate and other forms of local pollution, but we will ignore them, mainly because their effect is localised in the place of consumption and therefore it would be better addressed by local, not national or international, regulations.
- By the same token, we will assume that subsidies to renewable energies are only intended to avoid

a positive externality, i.e. the carbon emissions that are avoided because green energy displaces carbon-intensive fuels. In doing so, we will ignore other positive externalities (such as the avoided emissions of local pollutants) but we will also ignore the negative externalities deriving from renewable energies, such as the cost of managing intermittency in the power grid (Notton et al. 2018) and the potential impact on the landscape of large renewable projects (Schwenkenbecher 2017).

Other assumptions have been made in order to produce an estimate of the implicit cost of carbon. To begin with, we have used the estimates of emissions factors from each fuel (that is, the amount of CO_2 and other greenhouse gases that are emitted from the combustion of one unit of energy) provided by the EC's Joint Research Center (JRC 2017). That allowed us to estimate the amount of emissions embedded in a TOE of coal, oil, and natural gas. By dividing the net tax (i.e. taxes minus subsidies) falling upon each fuel we have found, for each EU member state and the UK, an estimate for the implicit price of carbon, i.e. the Pigovian correction to market price.

Renewable energies and nuclear power do not emit CO_2 directly hence, under our theoretical framework, they merely do not have external costs – which is not the same as producing a positive externality. However, each unit of green energy should, at least to some extent, reduce the use of fossil fuels and therefore contributes to abating carbon emissions. Hence, we have estimated the amount of abated emissions by estimating the emissions from the thermal generation that is displaced. That hides a further implicit (but realistic) assumption that most renewable energies are used to generate electricity. In order to estimate the emission factors of thermal power generation in the UK and the EU member states we have relied on the European Environment Agency's (EEA's) estimate of the emission intensity of electricity generation in 2018,[7] while correcting it to take into account that a share of the total electricity comes from carbon-free sources such as renewables and nuclear (which is provided by the EU Commission's DG Energy).[8] By dividing the net subsidy to renewable energy – i.e. subsidies minus taxes – we have estimated the amount of subsidies spent to abate one tonne of CO_2.

Figure 11 Implicit cost of carbon from energy taxes and subsidies in the UK and EU27

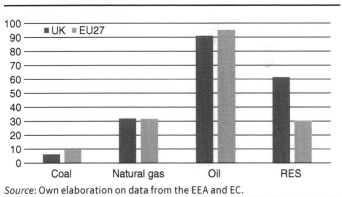

Source: Own elaboration on data from the EEA and EC.

7   https://www.eea.europa.eu/data-and-maps/indicators/overview-of-the
    -electricity-production-3/assessment

8   https://energy.ec.europa.eu/data-and-analysis/eu-energy-statistical-pock
    etbook-and-country-datasheets_en

Figures 11 and 12 show the results with regard to all forms of energy and renewable energies, respectively.

These figures are, of course, consistent with figures 9 and 10 but they provide a different perspective on the differentiated treatment of carbon emissions depending on the emitting or abating source of energy.

Firstly, these figures confirm the huge variability of the implicit cost of carbon, regardless whether carbon is emitted (hence taxed) or avoided (hence subsidised). Depending on the energy source, the implicit cost of carbon ranges from almost zero (in the case of hydro power in the UK) to almost €250 per tonne (in the case of solar power in the EU27). That is an economic and environmental nonsense: a tonne of CO_2 causes the same environmental damage regardless of how or why it is generated, and its abatement results in the same environmental benefit.

Figure 12 Implicit cost of carbon from energy taxes and subsidies to renewable energies in the UK and EU27

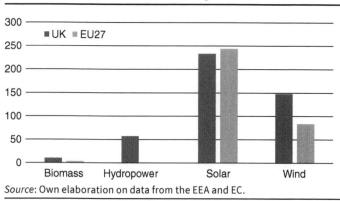

Source: Own elaboration on data from the EEA and EC.

Secondly, the most carbon-intensive source of energy, i.e. coal, is also the one for which carbon emissions are valued the least. On the other hand, abating carbon emissions via solar power is valued much more than achieving the same result via biomasses or hydro power, with wind energy in the middle.

Thirdly, whatever the 'true' social cost of carbon emissions, they are likely to be under-taxed whereas carbon abatement is likely to be over-subsidised. That leads to highly inefficient government spending (or spending by consumers if subsidies are financed through energy bills). For example, if the social cost of carbon is assumed to be around €100 per tonne, then emissions from coal are grossly under-taxed – the price correction from taxation and subsidisation combined covers less than 10 per cent of the 'real' environmental cost. Natural gas is also taxed too little given its emissions, whereas oil taxes are roughly, on average, at the right level – though they vary between uses. Some green sources are over-subsidised: while hydro power and biomass receive subsidies lower than their indirect environmental benefit both in the UK and in most EU member states. The cost of abating a tonne of CO_2 by increasing solar or wind power is much more than the benefits it provides. In the UK, solar and wind subsidies are 2.5 and 1.5 times greater respectively than the social cost of carbon. In the EU27 only solar power is over-subsidised. We did not include nuclear power in the analysis but the level of subsidies awarded to the Hinkley Point C plant would also exceed the environmental benefit.

One consequence of under-taxation of fossil fuels and the over-subsidisation of renewable energies is that energy probably costs less than it should, undermining the incentives to conservation and increasing the overall costs of environmental policies.

6 CONCLUSION AND POLICY IMPLICATIONS

Economists have long argued that taxes and subsidies can be used to ensure that social costs and benefits from particular economic activities are reflected in prices. They are not the only instruments that can be used to deal with so-called externalities, but most economists would regard them as efficient in many scenarios compared with alternative policies.

Two problems can be identified with the use of such Pigovian taxes and subsidies.

Firstly, the government cannot estimate the social costs and benefits from particular economic activities. If it were able to do so, it would also be able to estimate private costs and benefits from economic activity and so central planning of the economy would be possible and efficient. When it comes to social costs related to energy use, especially those arising from climate change, the externalities that might arise stretch a long way into the future and vary widely from country to country. Indeed, many populations may benefit from climate change. It is therefore particularly difficult to use Pigovian taxes to deal with the costs of climate change arising from energy use.

In addition, the use of taxes and subsidies to discourage or encourage particular economic behaviour can lead to the development of interest groups that will work through the political system to promote their private interests.

However, we would argue that there is no realistic alternative policy and that the use of taxes to reflect estimates of the cost of carbon emissions and other externalities is the most efficient way to address the risk of climate change. The problems of using Pigovian taxes are multiplied if we use other approaches to reducing emissions.

Indeed, the problems of other approaches to reducing emissions are illustrated by the current policies adopted by most governments. If we are concerned about climate change, there is no case for subsidies for fossil fuels and only a tenuous case for subsidies for renewables. Yet, not only do governments subsidise as well as tax both fossil fuels and renewables, the pattern of subsidies and taxes is not related to the externalities arising from different types of fuel use. By way of example, a tonne of CO_2 emitted by a gasoline-fueled Italian car costs its driver as much as €430 (Ramella 2020), whereas the same tonne of CO_2 from a coal-fired power plant in several EU member states, such as Poland, is taxed close to zero: indeed, in some cases, it receives subsidies. In the UK, carbon-intensive fuels for road-use are heavily taxed, even after allowing for the potential externalities from carbon emissions. At the same time, fuel used by farmers, the air industry and natural gas for domestic use is exempt even from normal taxes such as VAT.

When it comes to renewables, policy is no more coherent. Carbon-free hydro power is almost unsubsidised in several EU member states, whereas equally carbon-free solar power receives subsidies of more than €5,000 per TOE in the Czech Republic. These examples from different countries seem to suggest that policy is almost random and not directed in any way towards the objective of reducing emissions. In fact, policy is probably driven by the private preferences of interest groups which vary from country to country.

Climate change policy is chaotic and this leads to inefficient capital allocation, undue financial burdens on the shoulders of consumers and higher carbon emissions at greater cost.

The policies adopted to deal with Europe's energy crunch and, later, with the effects of the war in Ukraine have made the situation even more messy and less coherent.

In this book, environmental taxes, subsidies and externalities have been compared by energy source by country. No country in the EU, nor the UK, has a tax system that deals rationally with externalities arising from fuel use. On average, we would argue that energy is taxed too little across the EU and the UK and renewables should not be subsidised. Fossil fuel subsidies should, of course, be removed. The level of net taxes that is closest to the 'correct' level is borne by oil, natural gas, hydro power and biomass – though the level of net taxes varies immensely by use. However, coal is under-taxed and wind power and solar power are over-subsidised. In this study nuclear power has not been considered explicitly, but it would appear that the UK has promised subsidies to the new nuclear installations in Hinckley Point C that are almost as large as, or larger than, wind and solar subsidies (Robinson 2013; Myddelton 2007, 2014). This bundle of taxes and subsidies made the pricing of energy less transparent and forced governments to follow contradictory policies to mitigate the price spikes of the last few months.

Decarbonisation has been established as a key policy objective for the UK and the EU. But economic efficiency, including efficiency of capital allocation, is important too. Indeed, if the decarbonisation agenda is to be followed, it is still more important to have an energy market in which scarce capital is allocated to efficient uses and in which carbon emissions are reduced where it is cheapest to reduce them. 'Getting energy prices right' – to borrow the title of an important book from the International Monetary Fund (Parry et al. 2014) – can help to achieve both. And all of this becomes even more compelling as tens of billions of pounds are spent to increase the supply of energy from non-Russian sources.

The lowest-hanging fruit in policy terms is for the UK and EU to remove all existing subsidies, including exemption from normal taxes. In the UK, the most significant impact would be on the cost of domestic energy, on which the full rate of VAT would be charged. The UK and EU should then abolish all the complex and opaque schemes that influence production and consumption with the exception of carbon trading and, possibly, some basic support for research. Carbon taxes should then be the single instrument designed to reduce carbon emissions.

True, more subsidies have been introduced while taxes were temporarily suspended in the aftermath of the war.

But this creates a window of opportunity to rationalise the overall design of energy taxation and subsidisation, since governments will have to figure out how to get back to 'normality' while keeping their decarbonisation promises and protecting the most vulnerable consumers.

However, while the economist can advise on the level of carbon taxes necessary to achieve a particular objective, there are three factors that restrain us from definitively proposing a carbon tax at a particular level. The first is that the externalities are hugely uncertain. The EU estimates of externalities probably overstates those related to climate and also includes non-climate-related externalities that should be dealt with in other ways. Secondly, climate change and the externalities arising from emissions are an international phenomenon. Unless there is international agreement or a carbon border adjustment mechanism, we may tax our own industries and end up importing carbon-intensive products produced in more carbon-intensive ways from other countries. Thirdly, the impact of emissions has effects across the generations. Mechanisms of measuring intergenerational preferences are subjective. These issues must, at least to an extent, be addressed and alternative policy approaches determined within the political domain.

What we are able to do is to indicate the most efficient way to reduce carbon emissions using a carbon tax and indicate the costs that this would impose on households. If the target of net zero is retained, but other approaches to achieving that target are chosen, the costs may be hidden, but they will be greater.

The principle of any efficient carbon-reduction policy is that the impact of a tonne of CO_2 is the same regardless of where it is emitted and who the emitter is. The 'polluter pays' principle provides a solid basis for a reasonable environmental policy: financial transfers or other regulatory advantages to specific technologies have little to do with the environment. They are just industrial policy in green clothing and involve the subsidisation of vested interests under cover.

There is then an important question of what to do with the proceeds of a carbon tax and the savings from reducing subsidies. This has political and economic angles. There are merits from both perspectives of trying to ensure that the redistributive effects of a policy change are limited – though, of course, those who emit more carbon will suffer more from reduced subsidies or increased taxes. Insofar as tax and subsidy changes affect consumer prices, benefits would generally be indexed to compensate. The main effects might therefore be felt by wage earners – especially those on low incomes. We would propose a mix of tax reductions that were proportional to income above standard allowances (such as a reduction in the standard rate of income tax), a reduction in the standard rate of VAT and a raising of thresholds such as that for national insurance.

We believe that the governments' reaction to price hikes in the past few month provides evidence that our proposed approach is not only economically sound, but also politically meaningful.

Many of our proposals would improve economic efficiency even if the impact of emissions were ignored. If we are concerned about climate change and the associated costs of emissions, the 1997 Labour Party manifesto made the point very well when it suggested:

> Taxation is not neutral in the way it raises revenue. How and what governments tax sends clear signals about the economic activities they believe should be encouraged or discouraged, and the values they wish to entrench in society. Just as, for example, work should be encouraged through the tax system, environmental pollution should be discouraged.

As we have discussed above, one of its main policy planks was to do precisely the opposite and further subsidise carbon emissions. We are now 25 years on from the publication of that manifesto and it is time to take this statement seriously. Alternative policies will be extremely costly.

REFERENCES

Acemoglu, D., Aghion, P., Bursztyn, L. and Hemous, D. (2012) The environment and directed technical change. *American Economic Review* 102(1): 131–66.

ACER (2020) *ACER Market Monitoring Report 2019*. Energy Retail and Consumer Protection Volume.

ACER (2021) *ACER Annual Report on the Results of Monitoring the Internal Electricity and Natural Gas Markets in 2020*. Energy Retail Markets and Consumer Protection Volume.

Adam, S., Delestre, I., Levell, P. and Miller, H. (2021). Tax policies to help achieve net zero carbon emissions. In *IFS Green Budget* (ch. 8, pp. 345–91). Institute of Fiscal Studies.

Andersson, J. J. (2019) Carbon taxes and CO_2 emissions: Sweden as a case study. *American Economic Review* 11(4): 1–30.

Barreca, A., Clay, K., Deschenes, O., Greenstone, M. and Shapiro, J. S. (2013) Adapting to climate change: the remarkable decline in the U.S. temperature–mortality relationship over the 20th century. NBER Paper 18692.

Böhringer, C., Rosendhal, K. E. and Storrøsten, H. B. (2017) Robust policies to mitigate carbon leakage. *Journal of Public Economics* 149: 35–46.

Borenstein, S. (2012) The private and public economies of renewable electricity generation. *Journal of Economic Perspectives* 26(1): 67–92.

Bradley, R. L. Jr (1996) *Oil, Gas, and Government: The US Experience.* Rowman & Littlefield.

Bushnell, J. and Novan, K. (2018) Setting with the Sun: the impacts of renewable energy on wholesale power markets. NBER Working Paper 24980.

Butler, E. (2012) *Public Choice: A Primer.* Occasional Paper 147. London: Institute of Economic Affairs.

CEPS and Ecofys (2018) Composition and drivers of energy prices and costs: case studies in selected energy intensive industries – 2018. Final report to the European Commission.

Coady, D., Parry, I., Le, N.-P. and Shang, B. (2019) Global fossil fuel subsidies remain large: an update based on country-level estimates. IMF Working Paper WP/19/89.

Coase, R. H. (1960) The problem of social cost. *Journal of Law and Economics* 3: 1–44.

Coase, R. H. (1974) The lighthouse in economics. *Journal of Law and Economics* 17(2): 357–76.

EC (2019) State of play of internalisation in the European transport sector.

EC (2020a) Energy prices and costs in Europe. COM(2020) 951 final.

EC (2020b) Energy prices and costs in Europe. SWD(2020) 951 final.

EC (2020c) Study on energy prices, costs and their impact on industry and households.

EC (2021) Study on energy subsidies and other government interventions in the European Union. Final Report to the European Commission.

Fischer, C. and Fox, A. K. (2012) Comparing policies to combat emissions leakage: border carbon adjustments versus rebates.

Journal of Environmental Economics and Management 64(2): 199–216.

Forte, F. (1967) Should 'public goods' be public? *Papers on Non-Market Decision Making* 3(1): 39–47.

Ganapati, S., Shapiro, J. S. and Walker, R. (2020). Energy cost pass-through in US manufacturing: estimates and implications for carbon taxes. *American Economic Journal: Applied Economics* 12(2): 303–42.

Gambhir, A. and Tavoni, M. (2019) Direct air carbon capture and sequestration: how it works and how it could contribute to climate-change mitigation. *One Earth* 1(4): 405–9.

Goulder, L. H. and Schein, A. R. (2013). Carbon Taxes vs Cap and Trade: A Critical Review. *Climate Change Economics* 4(3).

Heal, G. and Schlenker, W. (2019) Coase, Hotelling and Pigou: the incidence of a carbon tax and CO_2 emissions. NBER Paper 26086.

Helm, D. (2003) *Energy, the State, and the Market.* Oxford University Press.

Helm, D. (2008) Climate change policy: why has so little been achieved? *Oxford Review of Economic Policy* 24(2): 211–38.

Ives, E. (2021) *Pricing Pollution Properly – How Carbon Pricing Could Decarbonise the UK.* London: Centre for Policy Studies.

Johnson, E. P. and Oliver, M. E. (2019) Renewable generation capacity and wholesale electricity price variance. *Energy Journal* 40(5): 143–68.

JRC (2017) Covenant of mayors for climate and energy: default emission factors for local emission inventories (https://publications.jrc.ec.europa.eu/repository/handle/JRC107518).

Kahn, M. E., Mohaddes, K., Ng, R. N. C., Pesaran, M. H., Raissi, M. and Yand, J.-C. (2019) Long-term macroeconomic effects of climate change: a cross-country analysis. IMF Working Paper WP/19/215.

Kang, K. (2016) Policy influence and private returns from lobbying in the energy sector. *Review of Economic Studies* 83(1): 269–305.

Kealey, T. (2021) Don't be like China. Why the U.S. Government should cut its science budget. Cato Institute, Economic Policy Brief 4.

Kealey, T. and Ricketts, M. (2014) Modelling science as a contribution good. *Research Policy* 43(6): 1014–24.

Kollmann, A. and Schneider, F. (2010) Why does environmental policy in representative democracies tend to be inadequate? A preliminary public choice analysis. *Sustainability* 2(12): 3710–34.

Kramer, K. and Ware, J. (2021) *Counting the Cost 2021: A Year of Climate Breakdown*. London: Christian Aid.

Laffont, J.-J. and Tirole, J. (1991) The politics of government decision-making: a theory of regulatory capture. *Quarterly Journal of Economics* 106(4): 1089–127.

Li, A., Xu, Y. and Shiroyama, H. (2019) Solar lobby and energy transition in Japan. *Energy Policy* 134.

Lockwood, M., Mitchell, C. and Hoggett, R. (2020) Incumbent lobbying as a barrier to forward-looking regulation: the case of demand-side response in the GB capacity market for electricity. *Energy Policy* 140.

Lomberg, B. (2020) *False Alarm: How Climate Change Panic Costs Us Trillions, Hurts the Poor, and Fails to Fix the Planet*. New York: Basic Books.

Metcalf, G. E. (2021) Carbon taxes in theory and practice. *Annual Review of Resource Economics* 13: 245–65.

Mieszkowski, P. and Zodrow, G. R. (1989) *Journal of Economic Literature* 27(3): 1098–46.

Mirrlees, J. (ed.) (2011) *Tax by Design: The Mirrlees Review.* Oxford University Press.

Molocchi, A. (2017) Does the polluter pay? The social cost of pollution caused by economic activities and environmental taxes in Italy. Impact Assessment Office – Senato della Repubblica. Focus.

Myddelton, D. R. (2007) *They Meant Well. Government Project Disasters.* London: Institute of Economic Affairs.

Myddelton, D. R. (2014) The British approach to privatisation. *Economic Affairs* 34(2): 129–38.

Newell, R. G., Prest, B. C. and Sexton, S. E. (2021) The GDP–temperature relationship: implications for climate change damages. *Journal of Environmental Economics and Management* 108: 102445.

Nordhaus, W. D. (2017) Revisiting the social cost of carbon. *PNAS* 114(7): 1518–23.

Nordhaus, W. D. (2018) Climate change: the ultimate challenge for economics. Lecture on the award of the Sveriges Riksbank Prize in Economic Sciences in Memory of Alfred Nobel.

Notton, G., Nivet, M.-L., Voyant, C., Paoli, C., Darras, C., Motte, F. and Fouilloy, A. (2018) Intermittent and stochastic character of renewable energy sources: consequences, cost of intermittence and benefit of forecasting. *Renewable and Sustainable Energy Reviews* 87: 96–105.

Olsen, E. L. (2015) The financial and environmental costs and benefits for Norwegian electric car subsidies: are they good public policy? *International Journal of Technology, Policy and Management* 15(3): 277–96.

Ostrom, E. (1990) *Governing the Commons*. Cambridge University Press.

Ostrom, E. (2012) *The Future of the Commons Beyond Market Failure and Government Regulation*. Occasional Paper 148. London: Institute of Econmic Affairs.

Parry, I. W. H., Heine, D., Lis, E. and Shanjun, L. (2014) *Getting Energy Prices Right: From Principle to Practice*. International Monetary Fund.

Parry, I. W. H., Black, S. and Vernon, N. (2021) Still not getting energy prices right: a global and country update of fossil fuel subsidies. IMF Working Paper WP/21/236.

Pennington, M. (2021) Hayek on complexity, uncertainty and pandemic response. *Review of Austrian Economics* 34: 203–20.

Pielke, R. and Ritchie, J. (2020) Systemic misuse of scenarios in climate research and assessment (21 April 2020: https://ssrn.com/abstract=3581777 or http://dx.doi.org/10.2139/ssrn.3581777).

Pigou, A. C. (1932) [1920] *The Economics of Welfare*. Macmillan.

Ramella, F. (2020) Benzina e gasolio: furono veri sussidi? Discussion Paper 1. Bridges Research.

Rentschler, J. and Bazilian, M. (2017) Reforming fossil fuel subsidies: drivers, barriers and the state of progress. *Climate Policy* 17: 7891–914.

Robinson, C. (2013) *From Nationalisation to State Control. The Return of Centralised Energy Planning*. London: Institute of Economic Affairs.

Schwenkenbecher, A. (2017) What is wrong with nimbys? Renewable energy, landscape impacts and incommensurable values. *Environmental Values* 26(6): 711–32.

Seely, A. (2019) Taxing aviation duel. House of Commons Library, Briefing Paper 523.

Sgaravatti, G., Tagliapietra, S. and Zachmann, G. (2021) National policies to shield consumers from rising energy prices. Bruegel Datasets (https://www.bruegel.org/publications/dat asets/national-policies-to-shield-consumers-from-rising-en ergy-prices/).

Skonhoft, A. and Holtsmark, B. (2014) The Norwegian support and subsidy of electric cars. Should it be adopted by other countries? Working Paper Series 15814, Department of Economics, Norwegian University of Science and Technology.

Somin, I. (2020) *Free to Move.* Oxford University Press.

Stagnaro, C. (2015) *Power Cut? How the EU Is Pulling the Plug on Electricity Markets.* London: Institute of Economic Affairs.

Stagnaro, C. (2020) A European carbon border adjustment mechanism: the devil is in the detail. Epicenter Briefing, 7 October.

Stern, N. H. (2007). *The Economics of Climate Change: The Stern Review.* Cambridge University Press.

Stigler, G. J. (1971) The theory of economic regulation. *Bell Journal of Economics and Management Science* 2(1): 3–21.

Sung, B. (2019) Do government subsidies promote firm-level innovation? Evidence from the Korean renewable energy technology industry. *Energy Policy* 132: 1333–44.

Tol, R. (2018). The economic impacts of climate change. *Review of Environmental Economics and Policy* 12(1).

Tol, R. (2021a) Estimates of the social cost of carbon have not changed over time. Working Paper Series 08-2021, Department of Economics, University of Sussex Business School.

Tol, R. (2021b) Do climate dynamics matter for economics? *Nature Climate Change* 11: 802–3.

Trinomics (2020) Study on energy prices, costs and subsidies and their impact on industry and households. Final Report to the European Commission.

Umit, R. and Schaffer, L. M. (2020) Attitudes towards carbon taxes across Europe: the role of perceived uncertainty and self-interest. *Energy Policy* 140: 111385.

Wagner, G. and Weitzman, M. L. (2015) *Climate Shock: The Economic Consequences of a Hotter Planet.* Princeton University Press.

Weitzman, M. L. (1974) Price vs quantities. *Review of Economic Studies* 41(4): 477–91.

Wellings, R. (2012) *Time to Excise Fuel Duty.* Current Controversies number 39. London: Institute of Economic Affairs.

Wooders, M. H. (1999) Multijurisdictional economies, the Tiebout Hypothesis, and sorting. *PNAS* 96(19): 10585–87.

Yandle, B. (2010) Bootleggers and Baptists in the theory of regulation. *Jerusalem Papers in Regulation and Governance* 9.

ABOUT THE IEA

The Institute is a research and educational charity (No. CC 235 351), limited by guarantee. Its mission is to improve understanding of the fundamental institutions of a free society by analysing and expounding the role of markets in solving economic and social problems.

The IEA achieves its mission by:

- a high-quality publishing programme
- conferences, seminars, lectures and other events
- outreach to school and college students
- brokering media introductions and appearances

The IEA, which was established in 1955 by the late Sir Antony Fisher, is an educational charity, not a political organisation. It is independent of any political party or group and does not carry on activities intended to affect support for any political party or candidate in any election or referendum, or at any other time. It is financed by sales of publications, conference fees and voluntary donations.

In addition to its main series of publications, the IEA also publishes (jointly with the University of Buckingham), *Economic Affairs*.

The IEA is aided in its work by a distinguished international Academic Advisory Council and an eminent panel of Honorary Fellows. Together with other academics, they review prospective IEA publications, their comments being passed on anonymously to authors. All IEA papers are therefore subject to the same rigorous independent refereeing process as used by leading academic journals.

IEA publications enjoy widespread classroom use and course adoptions in schools and universities. They are also sold throughout the world and often translated/reprinted.

Since 1974 the IEA has helped to create a worldwide network of 100 similar institutions in over 70 countries. They are all independent but share the IEA's mission.

Views expressed in the IEA's publications are those of the authors, not those of the Institute (which has no corporate view), its Managing Trustees, Academic Advisory Council members or senior staff.

Members of the Institute's Academic Advisory Council, Honorary Fellows, Trustees and Staff are listed on the following page.

The Institute gratefully acknowledges financial support for its publications programme and other work from a generous benefaction by the late Professor Ronald Coase.

Other books recently published by the IEA include:

Education, War and Peace: The Surprising Success of Private Schools in War-Torn Countries
James Tooley and David Longfield
ISBN 978-0-255-36746-2; £10.00

Killjoys: A Critique of Paternalism
Christopher Snowdon
ISBN 978-0-255-36749-3; £12.50

Financial Stability without Central Banks
George Selgin, Kevin Dowd and Mathieu Bédard
ISBN 978-0-255-36752-3; £10.00

Against the Grain: Insights from an Economic Contrarian
Paul Ormerod
ISBN 978-0-255-36755-4; £15.00

Ayn Rand: An Introduction
Eamonn Butler
ISBN 978-0-255-36764-6; £12.50

Capitalism: An Introduction
Eamonn Butler
ISBN 978-0-255-36758-5; £12.50

Opting Out: Conscience and Cooperation in a Pluralistic Society
David S. Oderberg
ISBN 978-0-255-36761-5; £12.50

Getting the Measure of Money: A Critical Assessment of UK Monetary Indicators
Anthony J. Evans
ISBN 978-0-255-36767-7; £12.50

Socialism: The Failed Idea That Never Dies
Kristian Niemietz
ISBN 978-0-255-36770-7; £17.50

Top Dogs and Fat Cats: The Debate on High Pay
Edited by J. R. Shackleton
ISBN 978-0-255-36773-8; £15.00

School Choice around the World ... And the Lessons We Can Learn
Edited by Pauline Dixon and Steve Humble
ISBN 978-0-255-36779-0; £15.00

School of Thought: 101 Great Liberal Thinkers
Eamonn Butler
ISBN 978-0-255-36776-9; £12.50

Raising the Roof: How to Solve the United Kingdom's Housing Crisis
Edited by Jacob Rees-Mogg and Radomir Tylecote
ISBN 978-0-255-36782-0; £12.50

How Many Light Bulbs Does It Take to Change the World?
Matt Ridley and Stephen Davies
ISBN 978-0-255-36785-1; £10.00

The Henry Fords of Healthcare ... Lessons the West Can Learn from the East
Nima Sanandaji
ISBN 978-0-255-36788-2; £10.00

An Introduction to Entrepreneurship
Eamonn Butler
ISBN 978-0-255-36794-3; £12.50

An Introduction to Democracy
Eamonn Butler
ISBN 978-0-255-36797-4; £12.50

Having Your Say: Threats to Free Speech in the 21st Century
Edited by J. R. Shackleton
ISBN 978-0-255-36800-1; £17.50

The Sharing Economy: Its Pitfalls and Promises
Michael C. Munger
ISBN 978-0-255-36791-2; £12.50

An Introduction to Trade and Globalisation
Eamonn Butler
ISBN 978-0-255-36803-2; £12.50

Why Free Speech Matters
Jamie Whyte
ISBN 978-0-255-36806-3; £10.00

The People Paradox: Does the World Have Too Many or Too Few People?
Steven E. Landsburg and Stephen Davies
ISBN 978-0-255-36809-4; £10.00

An Introduction to Economic Inequality
Eamonn Butler
ISBN 978-0-255-36815-5; £10.00

Other IEA publications

Comprehensive information on other publications and the wider work of the IEA can be found at www.iea.org.uk. To order any publication please see below.

Personal customers

Orders from personal customers should be directed to the IEA:

IEA
2 Lord North Street
FREEPOST LON10168
London SW1P 3YZ
Tel: 020 7799 8911, Fax: 020 7799 2137
Email: sales@iea.org.uk

Trade customers

All orders from the book trade should be directed to the IEA's distributor:

NBN International (IEA Orders)
Orders Dept.
NBN International
10 Thornbury Road
Plymouth PL6 7PP
Tel: 01752 202301, Fax: 01752 202333
Email: orders@nbninternational.com

IEA subscriptions

The IEA also offers a subscription service to its publications. For a single annual payment (currently £42.00 in the UK), subscribers receive every monograph the IEA publishes. For more information please contact:

Subscriptions
IEA
2 Lord North Street
FREEPOST LON10168
London SW1P 3YZ
Tel: 020 7799 8911, Fax: 020 7799 2137
Email: accounts@iea.org.uk

Notes

Notes

Notes

Notes